RENVOI

BUSINESS
MANAGEMENT CASES

RENVOI

BUSINESS MANAGEMENT CASES

DR. SANJEEV BANSAL
DR. ANUPAMA RAJESH
HAVISH MADHVAPATY
ANUPAM SEN

PARTRIDGE

To order additional copies of this book, contact
Partridge India
000 800 10062 62
orders.india@partridgepublishing.com

www.partridgepublishing.com/india

CONTENTS

STARTUPS AND ENTREPRENEURSHIP

PREFACE

The book "RENVOI: Business Management Cases" is a result of the authors' attempt to highlight dynamic requirements of the current business ecosystem. Realizing that real world problems are usually interdisciplinary, the authors have synthesized diverse case studies and learnings. Experts from various fields across academia and corporate world have contributed to the content of the book.

The book is a selection of the best case studies presented at International Case Study Competition titled RENVOI, held at Amity Business School, Amity University Uttar Pradesh in September 2016.

The case studies encompass a wide array of topics, and the diversity of themes will ensure that every reader — management students, scholars, and executives — will have something to gain. The compendium has been expertly edited by Dr. Sanjeev Bansal, Dean, Faculty of Management Studies, and Director and Head of Amity Business School, Amity University Uttar Pradesh; and Dr. Anupama Rajesh, Associate Professor and Head of Case Study Centre at Amity Business School, Amity University Uttar Pradesh. They have been capably assisted by Havish Madhvapaty and Anupam Sen, who brought their extensive corporate experience to bring a real world perspective to theoretical concepts. The diversity of experience of the authors has contributed to the efficacy of this compendium.

The authors thank the various contributors and experts for their invaluable inputs. The authors would like to mention Ms. Jasmine Khan for her help. The authors also offer their deepest and sincere gratefulness to the Almighty for inspiring and guiding them.

The Authors

Section

Strategy

Phoenix: Business Rejuvenation

Author Bio

Rohit Arora

Rohit Arora is Sr. Vice President and Head of India Region of the Global Enterprise Business for Tata Communications. Previously Rohit was the Global Head of Business Development at Tata Communications Transformation Services.

In a career spanning over 27 years of experience, he has served in premier Indian and US MNC companies such as Wipro, AT&T, Sprint and Tata Communications. As a business leader, he has multi-faceted experience having served in various functions and roles that include Country Head, Sales Head, Business Development, Product Management, Global Partnership, Customer Experience, Service Management, Organization Development and Talent Management. The above exposure has given him a well-rounded experience of all aspects of running a business in the ICT industry in a global format.

Rohit has B.Tech in Electronics from IIT BHU Varanasi and PGCGM from IIM Kolkata. He is also a certified executive coach from the Neuroleadership Institute, and uses his experience to coach senior business executives.

Sakshi Arora

Sakshi is presently pursuing her MBA in Human Resources from Amity Business School, Noida. She has done her graduation in B.com (Hons) from the University of Delhi. She volunteered with an NGO during her graduation.

INTRODUCTION

ABC Ltd. is in the business of providing transformation services to Telecom Service Providers (TSPs) worldwide. It is a wholly owned subsidiary of a global telecom major and has successfully leveraged its telecom heritage to provide quality outsourcing and transformation services to key customers across the world. The company started operations successfully, winning a large outsourcing deal from a well-known UK based TSP. This got it the visibility and momentum. The team at ABC Ltd. grew rapidly and began an ambitious plan for growth and expansion. The parent company had been in the telecom business for almost a century and had a wealth of experience in managing telecom operations. ABC Ltd. was seen as a great vehicle to monetise the operational expertise it had garnered over the years. It was seen as a great idea to expand its business. The quick initial success showed they had hit the right spot. There was optimism all around.

SETTING THE STAGE

The leadership at ABC Ltd. began hiring consultants that would help develop its expansion plan. Simultaneously workshops and offsite brainstorming sessions were organized. The company added a few smaller clients in addition to their one large client. The mood was upbeat and fuelled even more ambitious planning. The leadership began to spend more time on planning and lesser time on execution. New ventures usually require hands-on leadership for extended periods. Key leadership aspects were delegated, and consequently the efficiency was compromised. As a result, couple of years passed and ABC Ltd. was unable to achieve any significantly large deals. While the relationship with its existing high-value as well as low-revenue generating customers remained strong and profitable, there were not successful in winning business from new customers.

While the top-line showed no improvement, the leadership still showed a healthy EBITDA (Earnings before interest, taxes, depreciation, and amortization) margin by ensuring cost cutting and a cautious cost structure. As a result the bottom-line looked strong. In fact, the business head of ABC Ltd. once during an annual review with the parent company, said with almost a sense of pride that he seemed to have mastered the skill of how to make a company survive even without adding a single significant new client to the business.

The larger organisation at ABC Ltd. meanwhile lost its initial optimism due to a series of lost deals. As it usually happens in such situations, people started finger-pointing and placing blame on others. Soon the performance of various functions within the organization suffered adversely. Cross-functional teaming, which was an essential component for outsourcing business, also suffered. To win large outsourcing deals requires deep cross-functional teaming across various functions. Disparate teams across Business Development, Pre Sales Technical Consultants, Specialist Practice Teams, Delivery, and Commercial teams need to come up with innovative technological and commercial solutions. This enables a firm to provide the cutting edge to win in face of aggressive competition. It requires the energy, passion and innovative thinking across functions to be ahead of competition. All of these elements were diminishing in ABC Ltd.

Case Discussion

The Problem Continues

Unfortunately internal blame game took centre stage at ABC Ltd. Soon individual functions became more and more siloed. They began to focus on creating KPIs (Key Performance Indicators) that distanced their functional success from the overall success of winning new business from customers. While the small sales force was assigned the key responsibility of winning new business, the rest of the organization cocooned itself. As a result, some teams continued to garner promotions, increments, awards and other recognitions, even though the organization as a whole had stopped wining in the market place.

The initial success that ABC Ltd. had achieved was in partnership with a larger organization in the outsourcing space. The large partner saw value in ABC Ltd.'s niche strength and used its small size for demonstrating niche expertise, agility, and focus that on its own the large organization could not display. For ABC Ltd. the larger partner gave it the muscle and credibility it would need to bid for large deals and effectively fend off much larger and more mature players. It was a happy symbiotic relationship. The initial win had created a swagger within ABC Ltd. and this had dented the relationship with the larger partner, which now saw the fledgling ABC Ltd. as getting complacent, and soon distanced itself from the association. The leadership at ABC Ltd. made only feeble attempts to mend fences, and as a result the two drifted further apart. The overall Go to Market (GTM) strategy took a beating, as ABC Ltd. effectively did not have an operative plan to segment the market and create a win strategy in the market.

Morale Dips

Morale suffered and a large part of the organization felt disconnected and disjointed. The sales team was the worst affected, since individually they were neither winning nor earning their incentives. They were also unable to rally the wider organization around them to push to win new business.

The members of the leadership team at ABC Ltd. had each found a way to show success despite the organizational failing. It was epitomised by the business head's declaration with pride during an annual review about how he had mastered the way of surviving a full year without adding a client.

The parent company though, having floated the subsidiary ABC Ltd. with great fervour about five years ago, had after the initial euphoria not seen its vision turn into results. Despite giving it all the support, even after five years the revenues of ABC Ltd. remained less than 3% of the overall revenue of the parent company's revenue. With growth stalling and no real plan for revival, its euphoria was turning into despair. The CEO of the parent company at this point decided to give one last effort to revive the failing subsidiary by installing a new business head at the helm of affairs at ABC Ltd.

The Revival

Govind Pillai, senior management executive with over 25 overs of industry experience in the ICT industry, was signed up as the Business Head of ABC Ltd. as a last attempt to revive it. He had been with the parent company for the last eight years, where he had successfully taken on several challenges. He came to ABC Ltd. with a reputation of being a no-nonsense and tough taskmaster. His joining was seen as a positive change agent in the organization. His vision of organizational commitment, and eagerness to take up difficult challenges, was an inspiration for others. A typical Type A personality, he began working with the team. He spent the first few weeks meeting employees of ABC Ltd. across functions and levels, and talking to partners and past employees of ABC Ltd. to gather the pulse.

After the initial round of discussions, Govind observed the following challenges:

1. Re-working of Market strategy and Proposition was required.
2. There was an uneasy relationship with the key partner.
3. GTM strategy was not in place.
4. Morale was low across functions. Most employees felt either that they have tried everything and failed, or that someone else was responsible for all their problems.
5. Some functions were structured more for individual aspirations and dynamics; and were not designed with market effectiveness in mind.
6. There were employees across various functions who still had the drive to perform, but they lacked a leader with a driving force.
7. The current environment had given few employees a safe haven for their mediocrity to thrive. Their performance was sub-par but packaged in a politically correct fashion to escape attention.

Govind set about a systematic repair strategy. He realized that he had to work on various dimensions of the problem to be effective. He came up with the following solutions:

1. He used his reputation to his advantage to set the tone that he meant serious business. He openly declared that results needed to be delivered and mediocrity had no place to at ABC Ltd. This got people to wake up, either to perform or to find safe havens elsewhere.
2. In the first few weeks, Govind identified the top two opportunities that were winnable in the next 90 days, and put in all efforts to try and win them.
3. He identified the key fiefdoms that had developed in the bid management and commercial teams. These fiefdoms were strong and it was widely believed that no one at ABC Ltd. could do anything about them. To make matters worse, these fiefdoms were at war with each other and it was a tedious task to get them to work together. The dynamics were dysfunctional. While Govind tried to convince the head of the organization to break the fiefdom, he could see that the power dynamics were such that it was not going to be an easy task.
4. ABC Ltd.'s estranged GTM partner still offered support to the company.

CONCLUSION

As the team kicked off the new fiscal year in April 2011, there were several accomplishments in the preceding four months:

1. A large deal had been struck in the Middle East that had paved the way for a new line of business which was a relative blue ocean for ABC Ltd. given its telecom heritage.

2. In a dramatic move, Govind publicly announced the dissolution of the multiple fiefdoms into a merged group, effectively rendering the main actors of the fiefdoms rudderless. Given the widespread support for the move, the overall head had to go ahead with the decision despite his reluctance.

3. The relationship with the GTM partner was revived. A fresh partnership, with proper governance, was struck. This led to a positive sentiment to flow on both sides of the organization.

4. Govind had developed an overall strategy for revival in the market which he called the "4 Pillar – 3 Pivot" strategy. He had identified talented, energetic, and passionate employees across functions who were really looking to positively contribute to ABC Ltd.'s growth. Govind worked with them personally to bring them on board to sign up to the heavy lifting that will be required to execute his new strategy. These employees would become his torchbearers for the execution of his strategy.

5. Govind emphasized how each function contributes to the winning of business by giving a mantra whereby, "Organizational success was the only measure of success." He clearly set expectations, and drew a clear line of command for each function to contribute to organizational success.

6. A chief naysayer summed it up by saying that many things that had not succeeded in the past 3-4 years suddenly began to succeed in the last four months. The conversations in the corridor began to turn more positive, action oriented and with a "Can Do" attitude. A defining moment arrived during a conference call when the head of the technical pre-sales team, known for his cynical approach to business, thumped the table and declared "We must win this deal at all cost."

The "heavy lifters" at ABC Ltd. succeeded. The company saw many wins across multiple continents, effectively opening up a new line of business, opening new territories and regions, reviving its relationship with the partner, and reigniting the winning spirit in the organization. In the following two years that Govind remained the business head at ABC Ltd., revenues grew by over 180% and EBITDA by 160%. The CEO of the parent company was overjoyed and charted the next course of growth for ABC Ltd., calling it a key growth engine for his company.

SECTION

MARKETING

WHERE FUTURE MEETS PRINTING

AUTHOR BIO

Sandeep Arora

Sandeep is an electrical engineer from YMCA, Faridabad, Haryana. He has worked with Modi Xerox (Xerox India). A key player in the garment manufacturing and exporting business, he finally found his dream in the print industry. He has over 10 years of experience. He initially worked with the brand Cartridge World. Mr. Arora is now an integral part of the print revolution and is a leader in the endeavour to create a global platform for one click access for everything related to printing.

Chirag Prakash Arora

Chirag is a hospitality graduate from International Institute of Hotel Management affiliated with Edinburgh Napier University, Scotland. He holds a post graduate diploma from Pacific International Hotel Management School, New Zealand. He has over a year's work experience within the hotel industry specifically in restaurants, and has research knowledge in wine and wine marketing. He authored a paper in the area of service experience that was published in Pacific International Hotel Management School (PIHMS) Hospitality Research Forum News, Volume 3, Spring Edition 2015 (New Plymouth, New Zealand).

EXECUTIVE SUMMARY

This case study provides its readers with an analysis and evaluation of the current and prospective possibilities of the printer world. The method of data collection and compilation for this case study was market research conducted by Printodome and personal interviews with key experts from the industry. Results of this study will show its readers the prominent gap between the technological advancements in printer technology and the gaps that still exist in the area of maintenance and service. It will highlight the importance of integration between technology and service. Printodome's technology driven platform will be discussed, which serves on-demand as well as e-commerce services and products related to printers.

INTRODUCTION

Printers and print accessories have now been an integral part of our technologically inclined lifestyle for quite some time. In addition to office use, which already has a very high utility of printers and print accessories, home based use of printers has also increased significantly. New brands, manufacturers and distributors, branded or otherwise, are flooding the technological market. This is creating lot of competition within the market which is negatively influencing the customers as it is increasing confusion as well as trust issues.

Therefore, there is a need of an expert for the suppliers as well as the end users or customers. The expert needs to understand needs and dilemmas, and help by working out options which are cost effective, sustainable and time efficient. A brand should be such that suppliers are respected and trusted by the consumers, and the consumers also have utmost comfort of availability of product and service at their time and convenience.

In business and life, 'every dollar saved is a dollar earned'. The dilemma now is how to solve such issues where the market is scattered and the consumer desires a 'one click' solution worldwide.

SETTING THE STAGE

This dream of uniting various aspects of printing needs started more than a decade ago. Mr. Sandeep Arora, founder and CEO of Printodome became a member of the printer community under the brand name of Cartridge World, a brand well known for its cartridge and cartridge refilling solutions. Corporate usage of printers and print accessories was growing fast and was highly in demand as a hard copy of data was of utmost necessity. The home usage market of printers was being explored and targeted. Even then, the scenario in the print market was the same; there were multiple service providers, but no guidance for customers to avail quality product and services. Most of the customers, both corporate as well as home users, would only rely on international brands like HP, Canon etc. These multinational companies had a monopoly in the print market. They provided excellent quality, but the products were expensive and post-sale services were often delayed. On the other hand, small scale retailers, distributors and service providers were not trusted by corporate because of uncertainty of quality of product and / or service.

The idea of 'everything printing under one brand' came into inception in 2013 when Sandeep started on his own endeavour under the brand name 'Printer Bible.' Two such attempts were unsuccessful but the waters were tested and confidence in this project grew strong. The third attempt branded as 'Printodome' started in the month of November 2015. Help from outsourced developers helped boost this project in the right direction. Printodome is the only concept driven platform serving its customers with a comprehensive bouquet of on-demand as well as e-commerce services and products related to printers.

The key question asked during the process of planning was – "Is Print dead?" Several businesses have completely migrated their advertising efforts to the Internet. The internet offers several advantages, including cost effectiveness, potential for exposure to a larger audience, and convenience. Print still maintains its stance as a powerful and necessary component of an ad campaign. By taking a closer look at print media and some advantages it has over its digital counterparts, an article in Forbes identified the following points:

Tangibility – Print is physical. Magazines and newspapers are typically kept in houses or offices for long periods, while Internet ads are momentary.

Credibility – There is something about print that gives a sense of legitimacy. Pop-ups and banner ads on the Internet creates clutter for the user. Additionally there is the fear of spam and viruses. There is no imminent danger in a print ad.

Branding – Print ads are excellent for strengthening brand identity. Successful ads have a consistent aesthetic in terms of fonts, colour palette and types of images to establish brand recognition.

Target Marketing – Placing ads in publications such as specialty magazines can effectively reach niche audiences, which are typically more difficult to target online.

More Engaging – Consumers are more engaged when reading printed material, unlike websites, which are often skimmed in as little as a 15 second visit.

Less Print Ads – With more and more businesses relying solely on the Internet for their advertising needs, the decline of print publication can actually be used as a marketing advantage. Ad space is cheaper, and allow the ads to be shown with more prominence.

QR Codes – Placing QR codes on printed pieces bridges the gap between print and Internet. When scanned with a smart phone, the QR code routes to the homepage or a special offer page on the Internet.

The best way to market a business is to utilize as many channels as possible to reach every corner of one's target demographic. This should not exclude print. Finding the right balance between various media will ensure a steady revenue flow, and an increase in sales and new customers.

Printodome has been operating for more than a year now in Delhi-NCR and has more than 80 service providers on board this project.

Case Discussion

Present Day Problems

The last decade has not seen much change in the organization of integrated systems which can be utilized to create more efficiency in the print world. Even with the advancement of Internet of Things (IoT) and by integrating the physical world with the computer systems, there are several problems faced by suppliers as well as consumers.

Problems from the Supplier's Point of View

The number of branded and local suppliers of printer and print accessories within the market has increased significantly. It is estimated that there are nearly 2,000 vendors just in Delhi-NCR. This increased competition leads to unhealthy practices in the market. With the increase in local vendors and suppliers, there is no standardization of brands which are marketed effectively and well-known to the customers. This increase in competition creates a situation where there is no standardization of pricing of products and services, which in turn reduces the trust customers have on suppliers. Such unhealthy activities lead to no control on fraudulent activities undertaken by the small scale, local suppliers.

Problems from the Customer's Point of View:

With such uncertainty within the market, both corporate users and home users face a lot of issues. Trust is also a concern with respect to specific vendors and suppliers within the market. There is concern with respect to the trust on brand value of the supplier, the price demanded in comparison to the other market rates, and the quality of the product given or service provided. Most importantly, in the 21st century with a lot of work load and technological advancement, customers have limited time to tackle issues related to their printing needs. Due to such unorganized clusters created on the side of the suppliers, customers are required to spend an inordinate amount of time. It is a general expectation of the customers that, print being such an integral part of our lives, the efficiency attached to it and its services should be at par to the present day market scenario/requirement.

Other Generalized Problems:

In this diverse market scenario, the customers have an unclear understanding of printer products and its value added services. Comparing similar products of different brands becomes a hassle. This issue becomes more prominent when it comes to printer cartridges and cartridge refilling. There is no particular brand which has a hold in the market for refilling printer cartridges. Customers are still trusting Original Equipment Manufacturers (OEMs) for printer assistance who do not provide cartridge refilling options. Small scale distributors, suppliers and service providers of print services are marketing OEM compatible non OEM cartridge and cartridge refilling options to the customers, but again trust and brand related issues come into play. Taking advantage of this situation, OEMs are forcing customers to deal with sub-par maintenance and repair services, delayed availability and prolonged response to service.

The other problem which comes under the radar is the post usage disposal and recycling. Customers are unaware about the recycle or disposal procedures of the hazardous e-waste. Branded multinational companies are also not promoting e-waste management methods and techniques. None of these big brands provide clear information to their customers with regards to post usage / end of life procedures. Some of them who have units for disposal are just doing it for the benefits derived from Corporate Social Responsibility (CSR) initiatives.

With the advancement in technology, the need for expansion of technological services is urgent. The present gap between the two is creating a lot of complications and mistrust within the market and between customers and suppliers.

One Click Solutions

For such problems related to printing and print accessories, both for suppliers as well as customers, a one stop solution for printing needs is required for the convenience of the customers, as well as for the purpose of branding and standardization for the suppliers. This will help reduce negative competition and conflict between suppliers.

Printodome is one such platform which is a one-stop destination. It is the only platform in the market globally which is leading this concept for printers and printer related products and services worldwide. As per the problems discussed, Printodome provides its customers with expert advice on purchasing of new printers, provides information and shares knowledge on managing printers better to make the best use out of the amount paid for the product. It also provides customers with annual maintenance contracts so that any post purchase printer related issues can be tackled efficiently. This platform also provides its customers with onsite services with a guarantee of 4-5 hours response time, which makes their service very time efficient.

As highlighted above, the cartridge related issues were quite problematic for customers. Printodome offers its customers with trustworthy cartridge solutions, be it originals/ OEMs or compatibles at a competitive rate providing the same level of quality and performance.

It also focuses on providing corporate as well as home based customers printers and printer services on a rent / contract basis making it more efficient to manage printer and print accessories at an affordable rate without the hassle of ownership. Outsourcing of printing options are also offered to corporate clients who are looking for cost effective ways to get their non-priority work done effectively.

As mentioned before, the disposal and recycling laws introduced in the year 2011 were lenient and not effective, causing confusion amongst customers and the disinterest in the case of OEMs. Amended laws which will came to power in October 2016 have focused more on e-waste management and recycling. Pressure on product manufacturing companies has increased. Responsibility of disposal and recycling of the products will be enforced solely on them. Refundable deposits might be charges for proper processing of end of life printers and print accessories. Printodome is also focuses on lending a hand to its customers by integrating outsourced organizations which are focusing on e-waste management.

This highlights the altruistic values of Printodome, and the way it stays with its customers from the decision making process till the end-of-life of the product, and helps continue the purchase cycle.

Focusing on the supplier side, especially the small to middle scale manufacturers, distributors and local suppliers who tie up with the company will benefit from numerous advantages. Following the IoT concept, such integration under one head results in improved efficiency, increase in demand, accuracy, and standardization of product and service. There will be economic benefits for suppliers as well as customers. Training and growth opportunities will also be provided to the suppliers of Printodome as the platform has partnered with The Entrepreneurship School.

CONCLUSION – PLAN FOR THE FUTURE

Printodome is currently focusing on a three year growth plan, where their initial target of integrating Delhi-NCR has been successful. With the technological advancements growing rapidly, the aim of this platform is also to integrate 3D printing into their brand, mainly focusing on the medical advancements with 3D printing. Print technology in 3D printing has already made an impact in many ways like in small scale model designing and printing. An example of this is Weta Workshop, New Zealand, who have used this technology to create costumes and other artefacts used in Oscar winning movies. In recent updates on medical 3D printing, it is seen that the Food and Drug Association (FDA) has recognized, accepted and approved the first tablet printed by using a 3D printer. There have also been technological advancements in erasable ink printing. Printodome aims to be the priority platform for MNCs who intend to launch their products in the Indian as well as the Asian market. With this, it aims to be a recognized brand globally for everything related to printing.

ACKNOWLEDGEMENTS

This research was supported by Mr. Sandeep Arora, Founder/CEO of Printodome. We would like to thank Mr. Ranbir Singh (Legal processes and new business openings, Printodome) and Mr. Siddharth Samuel (Digital marketing, Printodome) for assistance with the whole process, and for comments that greatly improved the manuscript.

We would also like to thank Ms. Anamika Sharma (Business development, Printodome), the team of CHL (website and creative team), and The Entrepreneurship School for their continuous support towards Printodome and its future. We are also immensely grateful to the entire team of Printodome for their comments on an earlier version of the manuscript.

Last Mile Connectivity: Broadband In Rural India

Author Bio

Anirban Ghose

Anirban is currently pursuing his MBA from Amity Business School, Noida specializing in marketing and information technology. He has worked in the fundraiser team at an NGO and also has work experience of working as a process advisor. He was awarded the first prize at Conduit 2016, a case study competition organized by Amity Business School.

EXECUTIVE SUMMARY

Internet is considered to be the one of the most important inventions of the 20th century. The ability to connect different types of hypertext document to an information system is a remarkable achievement. During the late 20th century Internet played a major role in revolutionizing commerce, culture and technology. Although life without Internet seems to be an impossible task, there are many places where Internet is being used sparsely. Therefore, in order to connect the unconnected, a sustainable and affordable form of technology needs to be adopted.

SETTING THE STAGE

Research shows that accessibility to reliable and affordable internet connection is a self-reinforcing enabler for high standard of living. However half of the world population live in areas where Internet connection is sparsely available. Today Internet connects almost 3 billion people worldwide, as shown in Exhibit 1. Half of these Internet users belong to developing countries which have a significant economic potential. India is one of the developing countries which offers a notable example of Internet growth potential.

Exhibit 1: Internet Users Worldwide

Year	Internet Users	Penetration (% of Population)	World Population
2016	3,424,971,237	46.1 %	7,432,663,275
2015	3,185,996,155	43.4 %	7,349,472,099
2014	2,956,385,569	40.7 %	7,265,785,946
2013	2,728,428,107	38.0 %	7,181,715,139
2012	2,494,736,248	35.1 %	7,097,500,453

Source: www.InternetLiveStats.com

Internet in today's environment plays an important aspect in everybody's life. For some, Internet refers to a way of socializing and for some it refers to the way to conduct business. Others use internet for entertainment. Internet also enables an individual to do things efficiently and effectively.

Today broadband is not only seen as a medium to search for information; it is also used to guarantee development of economy and overall social improvement. Therefore, it is imperative to ensure that everyone is connected to Internet in some way or the other. However there are many countries or regions in the world where internet accessibility is very poor.

India is ranked second in the number of internet users worldwide. There are 350 million Internet users in India. However out of these only 289 million users belong to the urban population and the rest 61 million belong to the rural areas. The overall internet penetration is only 27%. There is a significant mismatch between the number of internet users in urban and rural population. Internet penetration capacity of urban population is 76% whereas the internet penetration capacity of rural India is 7%. Internet penetration in rural India needs to increase significantly to have an impact. It would increase access to information and lead to an improvement in literacy level, subsequently improving the standard of living. The true potential rural market is still untapped. It is crucial for the government to provide basic broadband connection to the rural India as it is still considered to be an untapped market. The Digital India mission launched by the Government of India is one such effort, which is aimed at providing internet connectivity with the vision to change India into a digitally enabled society and information economy.

CHALLENGES FOR RURAL BROADBAND CONNECTION

Connecting the population of rural India is not an easy or a straightforward task. There are several challenges that exist. Telecom companies are not focusing on rural connections since the average revenue per user (ARPU) is low and they do not have adequate number of prospective connections. ARPU refers to the total revenue divided by the total number of users. Apart from the above mentioned issues, there exist infrastructure challenges. Setting up of broadband connection requires towers, antennas, servers, generator etc. which involve significant costs. Moreover, a steady power supply and high cost of technical expertise adds up the list of challenges faced in broadband connection in rural parts of the world. Uninterrupted power supply is important as all the electronic devices in the tower require electricity to run effectively and efficiently. Technical expertise is required for constant maintenance and to rectify any breakdowns.

Digital literacy is also a challenge. The government therefore not only needs to provide internet connection but also educate the rural population. Efforts need to be put in by all stakeholders (government, telecom companies) to make the rural population digital literate.

SOLUTION TO RURAL BROADBAND ACCESS

Innovative forms of technology need to be adopted. These technologies should meet the criteria of low cost, low power and low maintenance. Wi-Fi hotspots is an example of a technology that fulfils all the three criteria. As it does not require use of wires and can be easily installed, it can be a perfect option to connect the rural masses. An innovative company named Witown specializes in connecting the unconnected population of the world using sustainable and affordable form of technology. The company connects the rural masses by using Wi-Fi hotspots in villages. These hotspots are capable to connect users within a range of 500 meters around the tower. The tower used for providing internet are both affordable and sustainable in nature. This new emerging concept is emerging is referred to as "everything on tower".

Usually setting of typical Wi-Fi hotspots requires building space, steady power supply and a tower on which the networking hardware would be installed. The "everything on tower" concept removes the need for the above mentioned requirements and physically puts every hardware on the tower in a secure and safe manner. The steady power supply is managed by solar panels.

The problem of limited spending capacity of individuals living in the rural sector can be solved through special microfinance options. These microfinance options can be provided to the end consumer enabling them to buy the necessary mobile phone hardware and the service connection. The applicants can be selected considering various factors such as the number of literate person at their home, account holder of a particular bank for a particular period of time, good track record of repayment etc.

Conclusion: Going Forward

The traditional business model for providing internet connection in rural sector cannot be sustained because the population density is low and the cost of service provision in the rural sector is high. Therefore in order to be successful an out-of-the-box business model needs to be adopted so as to balance out the high cost of service provision and the low paying capacity of individuals in the rural sector. In order to make broadband connectivity in rural areas a successful business model, all the stakeholders like government, entrepreneurs, service providers, regulators, NGOs and the government need to actively participate in order to achieve 100% internet access in India.

Impact Of Applications On The Digital Economy: Marching Towards An App Driven Economy

Author Bio

Sunil Gupta

Sunil presently works as PGT in Department of Economics at Mayo College, Ajmer. He has completed his MBA from MDS University, Ajmer and has done his post-graduation in M.Com and Economics. He also has a post-graduate diploma in Financial Management from IGNOU. In his previous roles, he has had experience of working as a Deputy Superintendent for conduction of CBSE examinations, and has also worked with Rajasthan Breweries.

Vatsal Sahni

Vatsal Sahani is currently pursuing his education from Mayo College Ajmer, where he has secured a perfect 10 CGPA in Class-X C.B.S.E Examinations. He was awarded the Principal's medal for excellence in academics along with the Mayo College General Council Scholarship and Mahindra Search for talent Scholarship for topping the batch. Additionally, he also scored 93% in DELF A1 examination for French and has secured 35 in ACT standardized test placing him in the 99th percentile globally. Vatsal has also attended the Leadership & Global Engagement program at Brown University USA.

He cleared the Trinity College, London Examination in Speech and Drama with distinction and represented India and Mayo at the World School Debates, Slovenia. He has been an ambassador to Mayo both in India and abroad through his experiences at the Round Square International Conference in Singapore, and for football in World Sports Festival in Austria and the French Festival in Pakistan. He is a certified Stock Market/MCX Research and Technical Analyst, and has work experience in the financial sector through his internship at Market Hub Stock Broking.

EXECUTIVE SUMMARY

The Indian economy has gone through multiple phases since independence. First it took shape in the form of an agricultural economy and an agrarian society. This was followed till 1965 when state economic policies of the then government led to a progression towards a more industrialized economy. During the 80^s and 90^s there was a significant emergence of some of India's largest conglomerates and corporates. In 1991, when reforms were initiated and sanctions were lifted, it led and shaped the Indian economy in a more liberal manner than ever before. This promoted free trade and changed the dynamics of socio-economic governance, in turn restructuring the economy. This phase of the economy recorded the highest annual compound growth rate (6.3%) since independence in 1947.

INDUSTRY BACKGROUND

A new phase that has been taking shape lately is the 'application driven' phase (technology). The impact of the Internet and technology has been evident especially in the last decade. The dependence and the immersion of internet in our lives has had a great impact on the economy as well. The internet bubble and the dot com boom were signs of concern, but this era has withstood the test of time. Technology has started impacting every possible field. Over the years, technology giants such as Google, Facebook etc. have taken charge of a significant portion of the economy. Originally when computers came into commercial use, it immensely benefited the common man. However, as years progressed and technology advanced, miniaturization came into play, and applications were introduced to the market.

In a developing country like India, price and affordability is always a huge factor. The mobile phone is cheaper and more accessible than any other technological device such as a laptop, tablet or a desktop. This led to a significant increase in the number of mobile phone users in the country. Smartphone usage has also increased, and the number of smartphone users in India continues to grow rapidly.

This rapid increase in smartphone users has led to an increase in number of applications being used. There are over 200 million smartphone users in India. The average smartphone user is observed to spend around 169 minutes per day on their device. Given the diverse demographic distribution of the Indian population, smartphone usage varies significantly. It has been observed that there is an upward trend in the time spent on applications by an average user on their smartphone. This leads to a big concern – 'data rates'. High data rates dissuade smartphone users from browsing the Internet extensively. While the technological advancements in the cellular industry in both hardware and software continue, lowering of data rates is imperative to increase adoption. It is expected that increase in data consumption will also lead to an increase in application downloads.

It is important to understand the economic theory of law of demand and supply. When advancement in data technology is introduced, it reduces the price of the previous technology, which in turn leads to an increase in the consumption. For instance, the launch of the Reliance Jio project in 2016 was met with enthusiastic response. The competitors have also had to play along to remain competitive. Every time a new technology is launched, there is increasing demand of the previous technology. The price for 3G is expected to go down substantially, thus reaching out to more consumers as well as increasing usage by current consumers.

CONCLUSION

Consequentially, the increased smartphone penetration and data usage will lead to the inclusion of applications in the consumer's life.

- FinTech (Finance – Technology) in a form of digital wallets. Payment portals are reducing the dependence on traditional financial instiutions.
- E-commerce portals have been competing with basic traditional businesses and day to day trade.
- Books are being replaced by online e-books that can be stored and accesed digitally.
- Farmers have started to use apps like 'Mandi Trades' that helps them find the right buyers by eliminating middlemen.
- Social neworking mainly takes place through the medium of platforms such as Facebook, Instagram, Twitter etc.

Ther are numerous other examples. A common thread is that they are are impacting and benefitting consumers. Using a completely virtual enviornment is not merely beneficial for the consumers, but also for companies as it allows them to reach out to a larger audience, and in a more personalized manner.

SECTION

INTERNATIONAL BUSINESS

INVESTMENTS AND INDIA: FDI TRENDS

AUTHOR BIO

Nirav Sahni

Nirav is currently pursuing his education in the business school at McGill University in Canada. He has corporate experience from working at Deloitte in their Financial Advisory and analytics team for two years. A keen entrepreneur, Nirav is active in the start-up community and is currently working on an e-commerce and big data venture called VRentin where he holds the position of the Chief Business Officer. Prior to McGill, Nirav has taken courses in Financial Statistics and Economics at Harvard University where he was ranked amongst the top 5% of his class and earned a recommendation by his professors. An avid learner with interest in emerging markets, he has attended and been invited to conferences at Harvard Business School and Columbia Business School. He has been awarded the Principal's Medal for Excellence in Academics at Mayo College, Ajmer and has also been a state level swimmer in India. His most recent accomplishment is the publication of his book titled 'Compendium: Management Cases from Emerging Markets.'

INTRODUCTION

India's approach to foreign investment has seen a great change since the early 1990's when the structural economic reforms were introduced and brought to the country. The Indian government earlier practiced and ran a very protected and controlled economy that did not allow free trade from across the globe. However, a new reform was set in motion that would result in a relatively liberal economy. The Balance of Payments crises at that time pushed for it and expedited the process resulting in a liberal India.

The commencement of the reform segregates the growth period of the Indian economy into two phases – Pre Liberalization and Post Liberalization, which denotes the period before and after the reform. In order to understand and analyse the impact and the trends of FDI (Foreign Direct Investment) on the country, it is essential to observe the impact of the reform and gauge if it has led to a positive or a negative outcome for the country and the economy.

CASE DISCUSSION

Statistically, the GDP was close to 3.7 - 4% before liberalization and has gone as high as 7.6% in 2015. The protectionist economy has led to the FDI policy being very cautious and selective in view of the import substitution strategy of industrialization. However, as times progressed, the need for becoming self-reliant led to FDI gradually starting in fields of high technology for national development; but was restricted to some parts especially in low tech areas to mainly protect the local and domestic industries. However, this did not mean that foreign collaboration was not taking place; it was just limited to and was only taking place in the public sector and government initiatives. It was intermittent in the private sector as government authorization was a difficult task which led to the nationalization of certain crucial sectors such as banks and foreign oil majors. This situation lead to stagflation and technological obsolescence in India which was leaving a negative impact on the economy, thereby restricting growth.

Realizing this as a major drawback and a setback for the nation, the restrictions on certain sectors and areas such as power, telecommunications, oil and natural gas was relaxed and eventually in 1991 the government finally embraced economic liberalization. The aim was to get rid of the stagnating economy, increase growth potential in the nation, and ensure a higher level of integration with the world economy. The new policy and reform led to an increase in the inflow of capital and funding in the country as the restrictions on investment projects were removed.

Exhibit 1 shows the trends of foreign direct investment flows into India since liberalization in 1991. The current policy allows FDI up to 100% in most sectors except critical sectors that affect national security and growth such as defence and petroleum. Overall there has been an increasing inflow of foreign investment since the past 20 years as seen in the data.

Exhibit 1: FDI Investment Flows into India

	FDI to India		Portfolio Investments		Total	
	USD (Millions)	in ₹	USD (Millions)	in ₹	USD (Millions)	in ₹
1990-91	97	174	6	11	103	185
1991-92	129	316	4	10	133	326
1992-93	315	965	244	748	559	1,713
1993-94	586	1,838	3,567	11,188	4,153	13,026
1994-95	1,314	4,126	3,824	12,007	5,138	16,133
1995-96	2,144	7,172	2,748	9,192	4,892	16,364
1996-97	2,821	10,015	3,312	11,758	6,133	21,773
1997-98	3,557	13,220	1,828	6,696	5,385	19,916
1998-99	2,462	10,358	(61)	(257)	2,401	10,101
1999-00	2,155	9,338	3,026	13,112	5,181	22,450
2000-01	4,029	18,404	2,760	11,820	6,789	30,224
2001-02	6,130	29,245	2,021	9,290	8,151	38,535
2002-03	5,035	24,397	979	4,504	6,014	28,901
2003-04	4,322	19,830	11,377	51,898	15,699	71,728
2004-05	5,986	26,947	9,291	41,312	15,277	68,259
2005-06	9,636	39,457	12,492	55,357	22,128	94,814
2006-07	22,739	102,652	6,947	31,881	29,686	134,533
2007-08	34,727	139,421	27,434	110,619	62,161	250,040
2008-09	41,707	190,700	(14,032)	(65,100)	27,675	125,600
2009-10	33,108	157,800	32,396	154,000	65,504	311,800
2010-11	27,829	132,400	30,292	139,400	58,121	271,800
2011-12	32,955	154,816	17,171	85,126	50,126	239,942
2012-13	26,953	146,582	26,891	146,559	53,844	293,141

Data Source: RBI

Source: Reserve Bank of India

While analyzing and looking at the main sources of investments into India, it can be seen that Mauritius and Singapore were the highest contributors with about 38% and 11 % respectively. The tax treaty with Mauritius allows or permits avoiding taxes, or having a reduced rate. This is the reason for high investment through Mauritius as most investors from United States and United Kingdom enter India through that route rather than directly entering India.

Trends and Impact

In order to truly understand the trends and the impact of FDI on India, it is essential to realise the key objectives and motives behind the liberalization policy. Government mandates indicated the main reasoning as:

1. Overcoming delay in public sector projects.
2. Clear the system of red tape.
3. Attracting fresh and foreign investments for the private sector.
4. Encourage accountability and increased competition that could lead to higher efficiency from domestic players.

Historical data shows that the motive has been successful, and the policies have helped unleash growth in India as this initiative is a mandate that has been positively carried through by all governments since 1991.

Looking at a sector wise analysis in Exhibit 2 in terms of the FDI flow for the past couple years, it can be observed that the majority of the flows are coming through the services sector with an average of about 27% for the past five years pre-2014. It has been speculated and can also be observed from the data that the pharmaceutical industry is on a steep rise, and is getting close to the service sector.

Exhibit 2: Sector Wise Analysis of FDI

Sectors	2009-10	2010-11	2011-12	2012-13	2013-14 (till Aug 2013)
			In USD (million)		
Services Sector	4,176	3,296	5,216	4,833	945
Construction Development	2,852	1,103	3,141	1,332	167
Telecommunications	2,539	1,665	1,997	304	10
Computer Software and Hardware	872	780	796	486	171
Drugs and Pharmaceuticals	213	209	3,232	1,123	1,000
Chemicals (Other than Fertilizers)	366	398	4,041	292	112
Automobile Industry	1,236	1,299	923	1,537	515
Power	1,272	1,272	1,652	536	120
Metallurgical Industries	420	1,098	1,786	1,466	114
Hotel & Tourism/ Construction activity	2,935	1,227	993	3,259	101
Total	16,881	12,347	23,777	15,168	3,255

Sectoral shares (per cent)					
Services Sector	25%	27%	21.9%	31.9%	29.0%
Construction Development	17%	9%	13.2%	8.8%	5.1%
Telecommunications	15%	13%	8.4%	2.0%	0.3%
Computer Software & Hardware	5%	6%	3.3%	3.2%	5.3%
Drugs & Pharmaceuticals	1%	2%	13.6%	7.4%	30.7%
Chemicals (Other than Fertilizers)	2%	3%	17.0%	1.9%	3.4%
Automobile Industry	7%	11%	3.9%	10.1%	15.8%
Power	8%	10%	6.9%	3.5%	3.7%
Metallurgical Industries	2%	9%	7.5%	9.7%	3.5%
Hotel & Tourism/ Construction activity	17%	10%	4.2%	21.5%	3.1%

Data Source: RBI

Source: Reserve Bank of India

This could be linked back to the innovation and technology in the pharmaceutical sector. International pharmaceutical companies are entering the country, increasing their presence, and shifting manufacturing in India. Major Indian players like Lupin, Sun Pharmaceuticals and Dr. Reddy's are influencing and attracting investments and investors from abroad. Moreover, automobile is seen to be on a growth track. The increasing population and high dependence on agrarian society leads to an increase in tractors, while both the agrarian and urban population are showing higher demand for cars which leads to promising growth for the sector in India. India is expected to be the third largest automotive market by 2026.

Having discussed and analysed the historical data of FDI trends and flows in the country, another key point of discussion are the benefits and advantages of liberating the economy. From an electoral point of view, it sends a strong message to the global economy and outside world about the growth potential of the country. On an economic front, it helps and marks the growth of domestic players as resources are now more easily available. Looking at prominent changes:

1. **Unrestricted Flow of Capital:** Free flow of capital between economies and nations makes it cheaper for companies to raise funds and calls for removals of trade barriers such as tariffs, quotas etc. Moreover, this promotes entrepreneurship in the nation as there are more avenues than the usual ones to raise capital. Raising capital is one of the biggest barriers for starting a venture.

2. **Improvement in Infrastructure:** Foreign investment brings along with it foreign players that benefit industrialization, which in turn reaches parts of the nation where the government cannot. This not only helps in reducing the bottleneck of investments but directly and indirectly results in the improvement of infrastructure in regions across the nation.

3. **Improved Stock Market Performance:** When investors / players from across the globe start investing or focusing on a specific region, the future growth potential for the stock markets increases due to speculation. The influx of foreign capital leads to an increase in number of IPO's (Initial Public Offer) per year as the approvals from VC's (Venture Capitalists) has been extremely positive for startups.

4. **Technological Advancement:** Opening the doors to the global economy not leads to infusion of capital but also a new and more advanced set of skills and technologies that result in development in a different and more efficient manner. This leads to technology advancements that make Indian companies and Indian infrastructure state of the art and globally competitive.

5. **Boosting Local Confidence:** Opening the doors not only makes it easier for organizations and people to enter the nation but also for local entrepreneurs / businesses to tap global markets. It gives them the confidence to showcase and present their ventures to foreign markets which can sometimes lead to higher returns compared to staying solely domestic.

CONCLUSION

The government has taken, and continues to take several measures for the continuance of the investments. Measures like increasing the FDI equity cap from 74% to 100% in the telecom sector has given rise and incentive to players like Aircel. Moreover, the approval of 51% in the retail sector has been seen as a huge step as the retail sector has immense potential to grow. The approval to set up JV's (Joint Ventures) outside India has become more streamlined.

Progressively, the impact of the trends and liberalization has made India a favourable destination for investments. The measures taken by the government along with the geopolitical standing of India, given certain characteristics such as democracy, stability in the political environment, large pool of skilled labour and low costs of labour, add to the incentives. There is still a belief that there is a better need and improvement for factors like improved governance and removal of red tape which would lead to faster approvals and sanctions, elimination of scams and promotion of Indian intellect.

The main factor as per research that have contributed to the preference is primarily the economic strength of the country which influences incentives in the form of tax cuts, subsidies etc. Other major factors are liberal investment policies, as well as improving social infrastructure. State incentives like land concessions can also have a major impact.

Further steps that could be taken are enhancing infrastructure facilities and logistics. An increase in state incentives and cutting tax measures always has a strong pulling force to it as well. Moreover, the most attractive investment avenues in the past have been through real estate, so a reform on that front or a new policy could help and build a long term investment destination.

FDI has had a positive impact and trend on the Indian economy. It has helped foster growth, integrate India with the world economy and made it a favourable destination for investment. As every argument or case, there could be a flip side to every situation. There are both advantages and disadvantages to FDI. The advantages range from the fact that FDI has helped economic development and increased employment and trade in the nation. It has led to increased productivity with tax incentives that lead to an increment in income that boosts and infuses capital. On the flipside India is still an emerging nation, so focusing on foreign investors could create fierce competition for very small businesses and local investment. There is a high inflationary pressure and a negative influence on exchange rates.

While buying into a foreign company or otherwise expanding business abroad can be extremely rewarding financially, the risks and negatives should be carefully considered.

Emerging Pharmaceutical Markets: An Analysis Of Vietnam

Author Bio

Subhasis Chatterjee

Subhasis works as Director, International Sales at ARIES EXIM PTE. Ltd. Singapore. He is an MBA from Anglia Ruskin University, UK. His role at ARIES EXIM involves the management of the sales teams across Asia Pacific and achieving the revenue targets. He is also responsible for development of strategies to maximize profitability across divisions and to set up strategic alliances with biotech & pharmaceutical companies. He has experience of working in the past with various firms including VISA and IBM.

Charu Sehgal

Charu is currently working with Standard Chartered Bank – Priority Banking Division, India. She is a Delhi University B.Com (H) Graduate and an MBA from Apeejay School of Management as a scholarship student.

She has more than eight years of rich National and International Experience. Four years of Indian Banking sector and two years of Insurance sector of Singapore has enabled her to acquire cross cultural experience.

Apart for practical knowledge of the financial sector, she has worked as an MBA Lecturer with Amity Global Business School, Singapore for a year. She was also associated with BMC International College, Singapore for about two years as Industry / Guest Faculty.

She has been a notable performer in Banking and Insurance domain and has won several awards and certifications.

Dr. Anupama Rajesh

Dr. Anupama Rajesh is Associate Professor and Head, Case Study Centre at Amity Business School, Amity University, India. She has trained for case study writing at INSEAD Paris. She has academic experience of over 20 years including international assignments. She has written more than 25 research papers and case studies for prestigious international journals and has six books and several book chapters to her credit. Dr. Anupama has also won several awards including the ADMA Research Award, "Shiksha Rattan Puruskar" and several Outstanding Paper Awards at International Forums. She also has a MOOC to her credit.

INTRODUCTION

Health is a term that describes a person's mental and physical condition. As a more specific definition, health is the state of being free from physical and mental injury or illness. Managing health on a national scale is one of the most heavily debated policy issues in many countries. Setting up a functioning health system is a challenge that requires the cooperation of many parties across public and private sectors. Health is also a large industry – health service industry in the United States create some 16 million jobs. The pharmaceutical industry generates nearly USD 1 trillion of revenue worldwide. That makes it one of the largest global industries. Pharmaceutical companies manufacture a large range of medicines for humans and animals. The global population as well as the life expectancy are steadily increasing. This, coupled with the fact that technological progress is very fast, makes the pharmaceutical industry relatively crisis-proof.

The 2015 CMR (Comprehensive Medication Review) pharmaceutical R&D fact book reveals a surge in global sales, reaching a milestone of USD 1 trillion in 2014. Forecasts indicate continued growth with the expectation of sales reaching USD 1.3 trillion by 2018. The pharmaceutical market is not in an "era of scarcity" as some analysts describe the pharmaceutical R&D environment post 2005. Industry data challenges negative perceptions and demonstrates the pharmaceutical Industry's continued commitment to creating and employing innovative solutions to tackle its biggest hurdles.

INDUSTRY BACKGROUND

Worldwide Pharmaceutical Industry

The pharmaceutical industry is responsible for the development, production and marketing of medications. Thus, its immense importance as a global sector is inarguable. North America is responsible for the largest portion of worldwide revenues due to the leading role of the U.S. pharmaceutical industry. However, as in many other industries, the Chinese pharmaceutical sector has shown the highest growth rates over previous years. Still, the leading pharmaceutical companies come from the United States and Europe. Based on prescription sales, New York City based Pfizer is the world's second largest pharmaceutical company.

In 2015, the company generated some USD 43 billion in pure pharmaceutical sales, while total revenue stood at nearly USD 49 billion. Other top global players from the United States include Johnson & Johnson, Merck and AbbVie. Novartis and Roche from Switzerland, GlaxoSmithKline and AstraZeneca from the United Kingdom, and Sanofi from France are the European big five. Branded, patented medicines by far make up the largest share of pharmaceutical revenues. Humira, an anti-inflammatory drug, generated nearly USD 15 billion of revenue worldwide in 2015. Oncologists continue to be the leading therapeutic class based on revenue. In 2015, cancer drugs made almost USD 79 billion of revenue globally. Other major therapy classes were pain drugs, antihypertensive and anti-diabetics.

More than any other industry, the pharmaceutical sector is highly dependent on its research and development segment. Pharmaceutical companies invest 20% and more of their revenues in R&D measures. The United States is a traditional stronghold of pharmaceutical innovation. The origin of most new substances introduced to the market can be traced back to the United States. Because of the steady loss of patent protection, the invention of new drugs is of vital importance for the pharmaceutical industry. Revenue losses due to patent expiry often are very significant, as can be seen with Pfizer's Lipitor.

Asian Pharmaceutical Market

Asia Pacific region is the third largest pharmaceutical market in the world after North America and Europe, with generics being the major driver for the pharmaceutical industry in this region, aided by factors such as the aging population and impending expiry of patented drugs. BMI's pharmaceutical expenditure forecasts show that, in general, developing countries will see a higher rate of pharmaceutical sales growth, while the growth for developed countries is lower. Countries that will experience strong growth include Vietnam (16.4%), China (15.0%), Sri Lanka (12.4%), Myanmar (12.2%) and Bangladesh (11.5%).

Pharmaceuticals contribute the maximum share in terms of volume, having evolved into a USD 959 billion industry that generates more than 60 % of the segment with growth expected to reach to 5.3 % per annum between 2012 and 2017. Combined sales of prescription drugs and over-the-counter (OTC) medicines are forecasted to increase from USD 277 billion in 2013 to USD 385 billion in 2018, representing a five-year compounded annual growth rate (CAGR) of 7.0%.

Asia's pharmaceutical sector has been expanding rapidly and in line with the region's strong economic growth, especially in countries of the Association of Southeast Asian Nations (ASEAN). The industry landscape of Vietnam's pharmaceutical sector is teeming with opportunities. The combination of Vietnam's expanding population, higher levels of health awareness, and increased access to medicines across the country should provide a roaring engine for the pharmaceutical sector's acceleration in the upcoming years.

ANALYSIS OF THE VIETNAM MARKET

Recognizing Symptoms

The domestic pharmaceutical sector is facing challenging structural weaknesses, the most notable of which are:

1. Entry barrier
   - Low affordability of medical drugs.
   - Widespread corruption among healthcare officials.
   - Inadequate intellectual property regime which hinders the future flow of foreign investments.
   - The menacing presence of counterfeits in the market.

2. Price Sensitivity
   - Inadequate price control regime, which leads to large price variances.
   - Chinese dominance.
   - Lack of a robust banking and logistical infrastructure.

Objectives

1. Analyze and understand the fundamental behaviour of customers in price sensitive market.
2. Identify effective market entry strategy (low cost manufacturing unit at Vietnam).

SWOT Analysis:

1. Strengths
   - Vietnam has been one of the fastest-growing economies in Asia over the past five years averaging an annual growth of 8.0%.
   - The economic boom has lifted many Vietnamese out of poverty, with the official poverty rate falling from 58% in 1993 to 20% in 2004.

2. Weaknesses
   - Vietnam suffers from substantial trade, current account and fiscal deficits; leaving the economy vulnerable to external shocks. Considerable 'off-the-books' spending clouds the fiscal picture.
   - The heavily managed and weak national currency reduces incentives to improve quality of exports and also serves to keep import costs high, thus contributing to inflationary pressures.

3. Opportunities:
   - WTO membership has given Vietnam access to both foreign markets and capital, while making Vietnamese enterprises stronger through increased competition.
   - The government will continue to move forward with market reforms, including privatization of the state-owned enterprises sector and liberalizing the banking sector.
   - Urbanization will continue to be a long-term growth driver. The UN forecasts the urban economy population to rise from 29% of the population to more than 50% by the early 2040s.

4. Threats
   - Inflation and deficit concerns have caused some investors to re-assess their hitherto upbeat view of Vietnam. If the government fails to curb inflation, it risks prolonging macroeconomic instability which could lead to a potential crisis.

CONCLUSION

The pharmaceutical market in Vietnam is expected to expand in value from USD 3.5 billion in 2015 to an estimated USD 6.6 billion by 2020. Vietnam offers immense opportunities to pharmaceutical companies. While there are several challenges, the opportunities far outweigh them.

FMCG ENTRY IN AFRICA: STRATEGY FOR YUMSUM NOODLES

AUTHOR BIO

Prateeek Mangal

Prateek works as Director – Client Services for SSR Management Consultants Pvt. Ltd. An MBA from Indian Institute of Foreign Trade, Kolkata and International University in Geneva, Switzerland, he started his corporate journey with Triton Management Services and worked with the FMCG giant in Africa and India. He is widely travelled and experienced across Europe, Africa and Asia and has six year of experience in FMCG and Manufacturing Industry. He has a passion to gather knowledge and is also a Diploma holder in Cyber Law from Asian School of Cyber Laws, Pune.

Prateek has co-authored and edited a casebook titled "Compendium: Management Cases from Emerging Markets". He has also been part of numerous Conclaves and Symposiums and has presented and published research papers on key FMCG and Manufacturing issues. He is also a prominent Social Worker as well and runs an NGO 'Neelabh Foundation' to finance studies of underprivileged children in eastern Uttar Pradesh.

Tushar Gavishter

Tushar has six years of sales, marketing and business development experience in fast-emerging consumer markets with top MNC's in India and abroad. As a global leadership program participant with a Singapore based MNC, he worked in challenging assignments in Ghana and Nigeria in different consumer goods categories, where he earned 'exceeded expectation' ratings and early promotions for stellar performance. Tushar started his career with Bajaj Auto where he led a team to launch Bajaj's motorcycles in Egypt. Tushar is currently pursuing his MBA in strategy and leadership from the top-ranked INSEAD Business School, France. He is an avid traveller, has lived in 5 countries, and is an adventure sports fanatic.

EXECUTIVE SUMMARY

Ms. Amandaine Kisiri was a young, bright and hardworking student from Kano, Nigeria. Amandine was a student with limited means but gets an opportunity to pursue her MBA in International Business from one of India's premier MBA colleges. Determined to make a difference, her efforts resulted in success and she got an opportunity to work for a national FMCG brand in India.

YumYum Foods was setup in 1999 by Mr. Tony Fernandez. It started its operations selling packaged noodles named YumYum in Guwahati, Assam in north-eastern India. Working tirelessly Mr. Fernandez popularized the product pan-India. Despite the success, he had not considering exporting the product.

This case is a narration of the determination showed by one employee. By making the most of an opportunity provided to her, she changed her own life as well as that of those around her. The case also highlights falling boundaries due to globalization and ease of doing business because of increased international cooperation, and how the so-called third world countries of yesteryears are striving hard and are becoming the business centers and emerging markets of today.

SETTING THE STAGE

It is a Friday afternoon. Mr. Fernandez had just concluded the quarterly review meeting of all business verticals of YumYum Foods. Performance reports were analysed and targets were set for the next quarter. Noodles and Ketchup verticals had done well in the review, however Jams and Preserves were considerably newer verticals, and were being given a slight preferential treatment by the management despite not meeting targets. The growth was steady for Jams and Preserves since their introduction three quarters ago, and they were expected to meet their sales targets in the coming quarter.

Mr. Fernandez's chain of thoughts was interrupted when the office-boy came and informed him that Mr. Sujit Roy along with Ms. Amandine were there to see him. Mr. Fernandez remembered last week Amandine had put up a strong case for Nigeria to be the launchpad for the distribution of YumSum noodles in Africa. He had requested both of them to meet him after the quarterly review meeting to give a final word.

Mr. Fernandez was still unsure – Is this the right time to expand? Will we be able to weather the storm that will follow by division of forces in two markets? Is Africa the right choice, and Nigeria the correct market to start with?

Case Description

Ms. Amandaine Kisiri was a young, bright and hardworking student from Kano, Nigeria. Amandine was a student of limited means, but a recent signing of a Memorandum of Understanding (MOU) between Nigeria and India for exchange of students for promotion of inter-cultural understanding between the nations gave an opportunity to Amandine to pursue an MBA from India. Foreign Trade Institute of India (FTII), New Delhi is one of the top ranked B-Schools in India. Brimming with confidence on her achievement, Amandine arrived in India and Joined FTII in July, 2014. After she joined the college in New Delhi, she was allotted a room in the hostel which was on college campus itself. She made several new friends and started her college life. One of the first hardships she had to face was food. The food available at the mess as well as the local cuisine was too spicy and did not suit her palate. After some experimentation with different everyday foods, she found instant noodles as a solution. She grew particularly fond of one brand - YumSum.

Time passed quickly with the rigor of studies, learning and blending in the rich and diverse cultural heritage of India, and teaching her own culture to the local students. It was now time for summer internship of students. The reputation of FTII had many prestigious brands lined up for selection of students. Amandine was excited and prepared hard for the internship interviews. She was eager to learn the work culture and ethics of the Indian market. YumYum Foods – the parent company of YumSum noodles visited on the first day for interviewing possible summer interns. Given her impeccable academic record and diverse background, she made the cut.

Soon she joined YumYum Foods for her internship. Amandine performed brilliantly throughout the internship and everyone was very impressed with her. During her final internship presentation to Mr. Sujit Roy, the National Head of YumYum Foods, she mentioned her wish to introduce YumSum Noodles to Sub-Saharan Africa, particularly her home country Nigeria.

YumSum is the flagship product of YumYum Foods. The company was setup in 1999 by Mr. Tony Fernandez, who started selling packaged noodles in the town of Guwahati, Assam in North-eastern India. The noodles had a secret spice blend originally made by Mr. Fernandez's grandmother. The packaged noodles were loved and appreciated by the people, and soon the product had a long list of patrons. Working tirelessly Mr. Fernandez had popularized the product pan-India but had not considered exporting the product. Exhibits 1, 2 and 3 showcase the growth stories for YumSum Noodles.

Exhibit 1: YumSum Noodles: The beginning (1999)

Stock Keeping Unit (SKU)	Price	Units Sold (In million)
YumSum (Original Masala) 100 gms	USD 0.15	0.23
YumSum (Original Masala) 100 x 2 gms	USD 0.25	0.11
YumSum (Original Masala) 100 x 4 gms	USD 0.48	0.35

Exhibit 2: YumSum Noodles: Today (2012)

Stock Keeping Unit (SKU)	Price	Units Sold (In million)
YumSum (Original Masala) 100 gms	USD 0.18	6.32
YumSum (Original Masala) 100 x 2 gms	USD 0.30	3.80
YumSum (Original Masala) 100 x 4 gms	USD 0.40	1.80
YumSum (Original Masala) 100 x 12 gms	USD 0.85	9.69
YumSum (Magic Masala) 90 gms	USD 0.18	4.60
YumSum (Magic Masala) 90 x 2 gms	USD 0.30	1.60
YumSum (Magic Masala) 90 x 4 gms	USD 0.40	1.32

Exhibit 3: YumYum Foods: Complete Product Mix

Product Line	Items	SKU's
Noodles	2	7
Ketchups	4	16
Jams and Preserves	7	7

Mr. Roy tabled Amandine's idea of introducing YumSum Noodles to Sub-Saharan Africa through Nigeria to Mr. Fernandez and the top management in the next board meeting. Upon deliberation they decided to move forward, considering this to be an opportunity to enter an emerging market and expand the business. As per their instructions, Mr. Roy told Amandine to prepare and present a report on the market potential and opportunity in Africa and Nigeria. She was told that a pre-placement offer (PPO) would be hers if she could convince the top management along with Mr. Fernandez on the opportunity in Nigeria. Also, she could be given the opportunity to set up the office for YumYum Foods in Nigeria depending upon her work on the presentation.

ANALYSIS

Amandine was determined to make full use of the opportunity provided to her. However, sitting in India she could only access secondary data. Her work was shaping up beautifully but she felt the work needed substantiation in terms of the market opportunity in Africa. She met with Mr. Roy and convinced him to arrange for shipping of an assorted carton of YumSum Noodles to her brother Patrick Kisiri in Kano, Nigeria. Patrick would conduct the blind taste tests on her behalf and share the first hand results and customer sentiments about the product.

After weeks of through research and careful scrutiny Amandine came up with the opportunity analysis in the Nigerian Market.

Report 1: Opportunity Analysis

Continent: Why Africa?

1. **Falling trade Barriers:** African nations are getting together for the collective good of the continent. Keeping in focus the growth, trade barriers are falling and intra-Africa trade holds enormous potential due to the proximity of the markets and similar demography.

2. **Changing Customers:** Customer purchasing power is changing. With the increase in disposable income there is an ever increasing middle class which has money to spend, motivation to try new products, and take risks with their choices.

3. **Population:** With a collective population of 1.2 billion and an annual population growth rate on the higher side of 2% per year, Africa adds approximately 30 million people each year. By 2050 the population is expected to double. However, it is a very young continent with a median age of 19.5 years.

4. **Disposable Income:** There has been a considerable increase in the disposable income of the regular African household. African women have always been in forefront working for their bread and butter. Dual income households contribute to the increased disposable income.

5. **Digital transformation:** In the past decade, due to the commencement of operations of different national and foreign telecommunication firms, Africa has experienced exponential growth in the private and public sectors. It is to be attributed to the increased internet connectivity and broadband. The digital transformation in Africa is gathering momentum with visible achievements.

6. **Increase in Infrastructure spending:** The state leaders understand that to attract more investors and corporates to their countries, infrastructure is vital. There is emphasis to improve the existing infrastructure and create new inroads.

Country: Why Nigeria?

1. **Abundant Resources:** Nigeria is a land loaded with natural resources – Petroleum, Natural Gas, Tin, Iron Ore, Coal, Limestone, Zinc and

arable land; most of which are yet to be explored. Nigeria is Africa's largest oil producer, majorly self-sufficient in oil and gas needs.

2. **Large population:** Nigeria Ranks 7th in the world in terms of population, with a total population of 173.6 million and a growth rate of 2.72% per year. Nigeria is one of the largest markets in Africa. The middle class in Nigeria is 11% of the population; most of the businesses are targeting the middle class nowadays which have a bigger chunk of their income to spend.

3. **Highest Population Density:** With a population density of 532 people per mile square, Nigeria is one of the most densely populated countries in Africa.

4. **Political Stability:** In spite of some periodic crises, Nigeria offers a stable political environment. In 2011, the Electoral Commission organized presidential elections. Nigeria returned to multiparty democracy in 1999. The elections were considered Nigeria's most successful since then. Nigeria is now increasingly being seen as the central driver of a vast African market by the international business community.

5. **Free Market Economy:** The government is pushing to create a business friendly environment through its policy measures. The thrust through different policy and programs is to push Nigeria to a free market economy. This will result in a very effective bureaucratic system streamlined to eliminate any avoidable delays which can have a negative impact on the business friendly environment.

6. **Fast Growing Economy:** Nigeria's total Gross Domestic Product (GDP) is around USD 521.8 billion (2013) and per capita GDP is a little over USD 3,000. The GDP growth rate is steady at 5.4% per annum which is higher than most other nations in Africa. A recent series of policy changes is expected to propel Nigeria's growth rate into double digits.

7. **Increasing Urbanization/ Improving Infrastructure:** The country is rapidly improving its physical and industrial infrastructure. There is uninterrupted power supply to commercial sectors and ports for transportation of raw material / finished products to / from other parts of the world. Air transport is developing. Reforms in telecommunications are making exponential progress. Internet is spearheading a 360° growth in Nigeria.

Report 2: Competitor Analysis (Nigeria: Noodle Market)

Instant noodles are one of the biggest consumer good categories in Nigeria. 60 million cartons are consumed per year, which is growing at 8% per annum. Exhibit 4 shows the projected figures for 2017.

Exhibit 4: Projected Forecast For 2017

Noodles Market size	2015	2016	2017 (Projected)
Volume (In million Cartons)	56	60	65
Value (In USD million)	648	700	760

There are over five brands in the market, as shown in Exhibit 5.

Exhibit 5: Market Share of Players

Brand	Market Share
Indomie	60%
Chikki Chikki	12%
Golden Penny	12%
Honey well	5%
Cherie	5%
Dangote	3%
Several Niche Noodles	3%

Indomie:

Indomie was the first entrant in the noodles market in Nigeria in the 1980's. It formed the instant noodles category and had 100% market share till the year 2000. After 2000, seeing the market size grow at rapid rate, other players also started entering the Nigerian market. However, Indomie still remains the strongest brand and has become a generic brand for Noodles in Nigeria.

Chikki Chikki:

Chikki Chikki entered Nigeria in 2005 with its 100g offering in noodles. Till then the only SKU sold in Nigeria was the 70g and 120g. Chikki Chikki observed a gap and was the first mover in launching the 100g segment. It was an instant hit and made Chikki Chikki strong in this segment. Till now Chikki Chikki is only present in 100g category and is a market leader.

Golden Penny, Honeywell, Cherie and Dangote Noodles:

Golden Penny, Honeywell, Cherie and Dangote all have their flourmills. Instant noodles are just one segment (small) out of their overall flour retail business. Hence their focus is not completely on noodles but also in flour, semolina, pasta, etc. which are their core businesses. They are present in noodles just to get a pie of the big noodles market.

The noodle players can be categorized into brand players and price players, as shown in Exhibit 6.

Exhibit 6: Brand vs. Price Players

Brand players	Price Players
Indomie	Golden Penny
Chikki Chikki	Honey well
	Cherie
	Dangote

Apart from two clear brands Indomie and Chikki Chikki, the other players are mostly dependent on selling through a price discount to these brands.

Current flavours in Nigeria market

- Chicken
- Onion Chicken
- Spicy Chicken
- Chicken Pepper Soup

- Beef
- Sea Food
- Cray Fish

Chicken flavour currently occupies more than 90% of the Nigerian market. Flavours other than chicken have a very low acceptance rate in rural areas. However, all flavours are accepted in the urban areas where people are more willing to experiment and try newer flavours.

Blind Taste Tests

Patrick conducted blind taste tests with mixed demographics in Kano and Lagos, the results were encouraging and approximately two-thirds of the control group liked YumSum over other brands on four different marking parameters – taste / flavour, aroma, appearance, non-stickiness.

Report 3: YumSum Noodles (in Nigeria)

As a new brand of noodles in the market, the USP of YumSum Noodles is that it is based on a traditional family recipe – a unique secret blend. It will be advertised as extremely popular among masses with very high standards of hygiene followed in the preparation process.

In taste tests done so far, YumSum Noodles have emerged as the popular majority in the blind tests, competing with the market leading products.

This should strengthen the confidence of the management in the product and the fact that it will be able to create a strong market for the company in Nigeria.

YumSum Noodles: Launch calendar

Given the current financial situation and company readiness; YumSum Noodles will be targeted to launch in Nigeria in June 2017. The pilot cities will be Lagos, Kano, Abuja, Port Harcourt, Ibadan and Kaduna. Exhibit 7 shows the tentative launch plan.

Exhibit 7: Tentative Launch Plan

2017				
	April	May	June	July
Launch Milestones	Finalize Venue	Product Ready	Launch	
Go-to Market Milestones	• Sales Team Form • Sales Trainings Commence	• Launch Market Mapping • Merchandisers on Board	• Trade Schemes Finalization • Logistics Deployment	
Marketing Activities	Marketing Preparations Commence • Messaging • Marketing and Launch Plan • PR/AR Plan • Sales and Customer tools	Pilot Program • Internal Training • Customer Researches	Launch • Live Launch Event • Social Media • Press Release	Market Activations

Report 4: India – Africa Trade Ties

India and Africa together constitute one-third of the world's population. A large majority of them are the youth. Their future will contribute to the course of this world to a great extent. India's approach to partnership with African countries is driven by the central aim of access to Indian market and support for Indian investments in Africa along with empowerment, capacity building, and human resource development of all participants.

Trade relations between India and Africa have a long and distinguished history. It dates back thousands of years to days when Indian traders and explorers, using the seasonal monsoon winds, sailed to the East Coast of Africa in search of mangrove poles, gold, gemstones and ivory. The traders brought with them spices which they offered in exchange of the commodities. Spices from India like cardamom and black pepper were highly sought after throughout the world over time.

Currently Africa enjoys a positive trade balance with India. India's imports from Africa reached approximately USD 19 billion in 2009 while the exports from India to Africa were only USD 13 billion in the same year, as per a report from the African Development Bank. India imports raw materials, including oil and minerals from Africa; while exports from India are mainly manufactured and finished goods, including transport equipment. Indian car manufacturers enjoy the lion's share of African Market. Industrial machinery and pharmaceuticals are also imported by many African nations. Nigeria, Kenya, South Africa and Tanzania are the major importers of Indian products in sub-Saharan Africa.

Technology sharing is also prevalent between India and Africa. In the past three years, about 25,000 Africans have been educated or trained in India. The reach of technological development is ever increasing in Africa, the advent of broadband internet connectivity laid the foundation of pan-Africa e-network, which now connects 48 African countries. It is becoming the new highway of regional connectivity and human development in Africa. India also has emerged as a major and rapidly growing source of Foreign Direct Investment in Africa giving tough competition to China. Trade between the two has also benefited from India's decision to offer duty free access to Indian markets to all Least Developed Countries in 2008. More than 30 African countries were directly benefitted from the ruling. Tourist flow from India to Africa is also increasing as Indians are taking more and more interest in the "Dark Continent" shining under new light.

QUESTIONS FOR DISCUSSION

1. What do you think about the opportunity assessment of Africa by Amandine?
2. As Mr. Tony Fernandez, are you satisfied with the market assessment of Nigeria?
3. What barriers (Sociocultural / Political) can YumYum Foods face while entering the African market?
4. As the management, will you go ahead with the launch plan designed in the case by Amandine?
5. According to your best judgement, will the launch plan meet its deadlines?

SECTION

INFORMATION TECHNOLOGY

IoT Security Considerations For Higher Education

Author Bio

Dr. Kamal Gulati

Dr. Gulati is currently working as Assistant Professor, Grade-III Selection UGC with Amity University, Noida. He has also worked as Visiting Professor at Stratford University, USA from January – May 2016. He has worked at Bahrain University in Kingdom of Bahrain as Sr. I.T. Faculty (Computer Science Department). Dr. Gulati has a rich experience of over 14 years in the field of teaching and research in Computer Science and Information Technology. He also has experience of working with both private and public institutions; as well as universities. He has several research papers published in national and international journals, as well as conference proceedings. He has also chaired various national and international conferences of repute and is associated with various International Journals as editorial board member. His current areas of interest include Big Data Analytics, IoT, Internet & Web Technology, Business Analytics, Database Management System, Data Networking and Advanced Excel with Visual Basic Macros.

INTRODUCTION

The Internet of Things (IoT) is the inter-networking of physical gadgets, vehicles (likewise alluded to as "associated gadgets" and "savvy gadgets"), and assorted structures; inserted with hardware, programming, sensors, actuators, and system availability that empower these articles to gather and trade information. In 2013 the Global Standards Initiative on Internet of Things (IoT-GSI) characterized IoT as "the framework of the data society". IoT permits articles to be detected and additionally controlled remotely over existing system foundation, opening doors for BETTER coordination of the physical world into PC based frameworks, and bringing about enhanced effectiveness, exactness, and financial advantage. At the point when IoT is enhanced with sensors and actuators, the innovation turns into an example of the broadest class of digital physical frameworks, which additionally incorporates advancements, for example keen matrices, savvy homes, clever transportation and brilliant urban communities. Everything is identifiable through its embedded processing framework yet can inter-operate inside the current Internet foundation. Specialists evaluate that the IoT will comprise of around 50 billion devices by 2020.

"Things" in the IoT sense can allude to a wide assortment of gadgets, for example heart checking inserts, biochip transponders on ranch creatures, electric mollusks in waterfront waters, autos with implicit sensors, DNA examination gadgets for natural / nourishment / pathogen observation or field operation gadgets that help fire-fighters in inquiry and saving operations. Lawful researchers propose to take a look at "Things" as an "inseparable blend of equipment, programming, information, and administration". Valuable information gathered is streamed between different gadgets. Current market illustrations incorporate home computerization; otherwise called shrewd home gadgets. Examples include control and robotization of lighting, warming (like savvy indoor regulator), ventilation, cooling frameworks; and machines, for example washer / dryers, boilers or iceboxes / coolers that utilize Wi-Fi for remote observation.

Development of Internet-associated computerization is taking place in several new application territories. It is anticipated that IoT would produce a lot of information from different areas, with the ensuing need for fast accumulation of the information, and an expansion in the need to file, store, and process such information all the more successfully. IoT is one of the integral components of today's Smart Cities and Smart Energy Management Systems.

INDUSTRY BACKGROUND

Starting 2016, the vision of IoT has developed because of merging of various innovations, including pervasive remote correspondence, constant examination, machine learning, aware sensors and inserted frameworks.

The idea of a system of shrewd gadgets was first talked about as far back as 1982, with a changed Coke machine at Carnegie Mellon University turning into the primary Internet-associated apparatus, ready to report its stock and temperature level of recently stacked beverages. Stamp Weiser's fundamental 1991 paper on omnipresent processing, "The Computer of the 21st Century"; and additional academic work, for example UbiComp and PerCom, created the contemporary vision of IoT. In 1994 Reza Raji depicted the idea in IEEE Spectrum as "little parcels of information to an extensive arrangement of hubs, to coordinate and mechanize everything from home machines to whole manufacturing plants". Somewhere around 1993 and 1996, a few organizations proposed arrangements like "Microsoft at Work" or Novell's NEST.

The idea of the IoT gained prominence and momentum in 1999, through the Auto-ID Center at MIT and related market-examination distributions. Bill Joy imagined Device to Device (D2D) correspondence as a major aspect of his "Six Webs" structure, displayed at the World Economic Forum at Davos in 1999. Radio-recurrence distinguishing proof (RFID) was seen by Kevin Ashton (one of the organizers of the first Auto-ID Center) as an essential component for IoT by then. On the off chance that all items and individuals in everyday life were outfitted with identifiers, PCs could oversee and stock them. Other than utilizing RFID (Radio-frequency identification), the labelling of things might be accomplished through such advancements as close field correspondence, standardized tags, QR (Quick Response) codes and computerized watermarking.

One of the key primary results of executing IoT, by preparing all items on the planet with tiny distinguishing gadgets or machine-decipherable identifiers, is to make a positive change to everyday life. A man's capacity to communicate with items could be modified remotely in view of prompt or present needs, as per existing end-client understanding.

CASE DISCUSSION

The Internet of Things Is Far Bigger Than Anybody Realizes

IoT rotates around expanded machine-to-machine correspondence. It is based on distributed computing and systems of information sensors. It is portable, virtual, and prompt association; and has the potential to make everything in our lives from streetlights to seaports "brilliant".

A sensor is not a machine. It does not do anything in a similar sense that a machine does. It quantifies and it assesses; to put it plainly it assembles information. IoT truly meets up with the association of sensors and machines. All the data accumulated by every one of the sensors on the planet loses importance if there is no proper foundation set up to do break down the data for data mining.

Cloud-based applications are the way to leverage on all this information. IoT does not work without cloud-based applications. Cloud-based applications allows deciphering and transmitting the information originating from every one of these sensors. The cloud is the thing that empowers the applications to go to work for at all times and at all locations. We have cloud-based applications interpreting that information into valuable insight and transmitting it to machines on the ground, empowering portable and continuous reactions. IoT has potential to truly play the role of a disruptor and influence several sectors in the years to come.

Applications

As per Gartner, there will be almost 20.8 billion gadgets on the IoT platform by 2020. ABI Research appraises that more than 30 billion gadgets will be remotely associated with IoT by 2020. In 2014 Pew Research conducted an expansive review called the Pew Research Internet Project. 83% of the innovation specialists and Internet clients surveyed concurred with the idea that IoT and related frameworks will have far reaching and profitable impact by 2025.

IoT will comprise of an expansive number of gadgets being associated with the Internet. In a dynamic move to suit new and developing mechanical advancement, the UK Government in their 2015 spending plan apportioned USD 486 million towards research in IoT. The previous British Chancellor of the Exchequer George Osborne stated that IoT is the following phase of the data unrest and referred to the underlying network between everything from urban transport to restorative gadgets to family unit machines.

IoT frameworks could likewise be in charge of performing activities, and not merely detecting things. Savvy shopping frameworks, for instance, could screen the purchasing propensity of clients by following their cell phones. These clients could then be furnished with exceptional offers on their most visited items. Different applications of IoT empowers home security elements and home computerization. The idea of a "Web of living things" has been proposed to depict a system of natural sensors that could utilize cloud-based investigations to permit clients to study DNA or different particles. Every one of these advances adds to the various rundown of IoT applications. Presently with IoT, electrical gadgets can be controlled remotely from the office. All credit goes to brilliant gadgets which make up a smart home. All this is made possible with the assistance of the Internet.

Utilization of the IoT is not just limited to these regions. Several other uses of IoT exist. The outline given here is only for the most unmistakable application ranges. In view of the application space, IoT items can be arranged comprehensively into five distinct classes: keen wearable, brilliant home, savvy city, shrewd environment, and shrewd endeavour. The IoT items and arrangements in each of these business sectors have distinctive attributes.

Trends and Characteristics

1. Intelligence

The basis for IoT does not begin merely with aggregating data and self-governance. Research in areas of self-governance and operation of devices is providing impetus to IoT. Research aimed at identifying changes in nature, shortcomings influencing sensors, and providing reasonable relief measures is expected to give validity to innovation in IoT.

2. Architecture

It is expected that IoT will require more than fundamental models. IoT will work as a part of semantic web, which is an extension of the World Wide Web and represents the next major evolution in connecting information. It enables data to be linked from between various sources. This data is then understood by computers so that they can perform increasingly complex tasks.

3. Complexity

IoT is a multifaceted structure with multiple associations.

4. Size considerations

The Internet of things would encode 5 trillion to 10 trillion questions.

5. Current and future IoT market

As of 2015, there are 12.2 billion IoT devices worldwide. This is expected to grow to 28.1 billion IoT devices by 2020. In 2050 it would grow upto 50 billion devices.

Revenue is expected to grow from USD 2.9 trillion in 2015 to USD 7.1 trillion in 2020.

Enabling Technologies for IoT

There are many technologies that enable IoT. A key foundation piece is the network used to communicate between nodes of an IoT installation, a role that several wireless and / or wired technologies may fulfil:

1. **RFID and close field correspondence** – In the 2000s, RFID was the predominant innovation. Later, NFC (Near Field Communication) emerged, and has started to be integrated in smartphones today.
2. **Optical tags and quick response codes** – This is utilized for ease in labelling. Smartphone cameras interpret QR codes.

Bluetooth low energy – Nearly all smartphones have BLE equipment in them.

Low energy Wireless IP networks – These are embedded radio in system-on-a-chip designs.

ZigBee – This communication technology is based on the IEEE 802.15.4 2.4 GHz-band radio protocol to implement physical and MAC layer for low-rate wireless Private Area Networks. Some of its main characteristics like low power consumption, low data rate, low cost and high message throughput make it an interesting IoT enabler technology.

Z-Wave – This is a communication protocol that is mostly used in smart home applications. It uses a radio protocol in the 900 MHz-band.

Thread – Like ZigBee, this IoT communication technology relies on the IEEE 802.15.4 2.4 GHz-band radio protocol. A key difference is that its networking protocol is IPv6-compatible.

LTE-Advanced – LTE-A is a high-speed communication specification for mobile networks. Compared to its original LTE, LTE-A has been improved to have extended coverage, higher throughput and lower latency. One important application of this technology is Vehicle-to-Vehicle (V2V) communications.

Wi-Fi Direct – It is essentially Wi-Fi for peer-to-peer communication without needing to have an access point. This feature attracts IoT applications to be built on top of Wi-Fi-Direct to get benefit from the speed of Wi-Fi while they experience lower latency.

HaLow – Is a type of Long range, low-power Wi-Fi. It is not capable to transfer much data (bandwidth), yet sufficient for simple devices that require a network connection.

HomePlug – This networking standard can be used to enable IoT communication over a home or building's power lines.

MoCA – This networking standard can be used to enable IoT communication over CATV-type coaxial cable.

Ethernet – This general purpose networking standard can be used to enable IoT communication over twisted pair or fibre network links.

CONCLUSION: SECURITY ISSUES AND GOVERNMENT REGULATION ON IoT

Concerns have been raised that IoT is being created rapidly without legitimate planning about the huge security challenges and the regulatory changes required. According to a Business Insider Intelligence Survey conducted in the last quarter of 2014, 39% of the respondents said that security is the biggest concern in accepting IoT development. As IoT becomes more pervasive, advanced attacks will pose a huge risk.

One of the key drivers of the IoT is information. Interfacing gadgets need to access and store more and more information to make themselves more proficient. Organizations therefore gather information from various sources and store it primarily in the cloud. This presents several security risks.

Current Regulatory Environment:

A report published by the Federal Trade Commission (FTC) in January 2015 made the following three recommendations.

1. **Data Security** – Organizations employing IoT need to guarantee that information gathering, stockpiling and preparation would be secure at all times. Encoding of information is required at every stage.
2. **Data assent** – Clients need to properly define the information they impart to IoT organizations. There are also protocols that the client needs to set in place in case of data loss or security breach.
3. **Data minimization** – IoT organizations should gather only the required information. The data should be held only as long as required.

SECTION

EDUCATION

Use Of E-Learning Applications To Promote Active Learning In Colleges

Author Bio

Dr. Rupa Bose

Dr. Rupa Bose completed her Ph.D. in 2008 from Jawaharlal Nehru University, New Delhi, India. She is presently pursuing Postdoctoral research from Institute for Social and Economic Change, Bangalore, India. She has participated in several MOOCs, such as "Foundations of Virtual Instruction", offered by University of California, Irvine; "Blended Learning: Personalizing Education for Students", offered by Silicon Schools Fund; and New Teacher Center, USA from Coursera in 2013. She presently works as Associate Professor in the Economics Department, Kamala Nehru College, University of Delhi, where she also holds the position of the Teacher-In-Charge of the Department of Economics. Her research work has been presented and published at various national and international conferences and journals. She is the principal investigator for an ongoing Innovation project.

Shruti Gupta

Shruti did her B.A (Honours) in Economics from the prestigious Lady Shri Ram College for Women. She did her M.A. and M.Phil. with distinction from Center for Economic Studies and Planning, Jawaharlal Nehru University. She was a Junior and a Senior Research Fellowship holder from UGC. She has over 12 years of teaching experience in the University of Delhi and is presently works as a faculty at Kamala Nehru College. Her research interests are Development Economics, Policy Issues, Comparative Economic Systems, and Political economy. She has several publications on different aspects of Indian Economy to her credit. An enthusiastic and popular teacher, Shruti lives in Gurgaon, Haryana.

Simran Bedi

Simran is pursuing her B.A. English (Honours) course from Kamala Nehru College, Delhi University. She has completed a 2 months internship with Edu4sure as a content blogger and a 1 year internship under an Innovative E-learning Project in Kamala Nehru College. She is keen to pursue a career in the travel and tourism industry.

Smriti Kaushik

Smriti is pursuing her B.A. English (Honours) course from Kamala Nehru College, Delhi University. She has completed a 2 months internship with Edu4sure as a content blogger and a 1 year internship under an Innovative E-learning Project in Kamala Nehru College. She has been a rank holder consecutively for three years at International English Olympiad conducted by SOF.

EXECUTIVE SUMMARY

University of Delhi is considered one of the premier institutions of higher education in the country, and the faculty members teaching in various undergraduate colleges of DU are highly qualified. Yet they seem unable to meet the needs of the present generation of students. The 21st century, with its revolutionary changes in information and communication technology, has put new pressures on the higher education system for the development of skills and competencies among students. The quality of education imparted by colleges and universities has often been a matter of concern. Active Learning refers to anything that the students do in a classroom other than passively listening to an instructor's lecture. In this context, a movement towards using flipped classrooms is gaining grounds. Teachers who have used flipped classrooms create content and post them to a website or Learning Management System for students to view prior to coming to the class. The class is then used to help students apply or practice the learning. Flipped teaching incorporates elements of online learning and traditional learning and is referred to as Blended Learning. Research shows that blended learning is the optimal method of teaching in contrast to exclusively online or face-to-face formats. In this case study the authors look at a Delhi University Innovation Project in which faculty members in a number of colleges were trained in innovative e-learning applications and the concept and use of Open Education Resources (OER). This paper presents the experience and the findings of this unique endeavour. It highlights problems faced, and the opportunities identified for enhancing the teaching-learning processes in the colleges.

SETTING THE STAGE

E-learning, though a commonly used term, has different meanings to different people. In the context of this study, e-learning refers to delivery of all, or parts of the course content, in a virtual learning environment. E-learning also includes use of applications and devices such as Internet, computer, mobile phone, video etc. to support teaching and learning activities.

Early interest in e-learning focused around its potential to teach large numbers of people. Whereas traditional education methods are limited by physical constraints, the virtual world has no such limits. Universities have also been investing in technology systems based on the conviction that technology can improve the teaching and learning experience significantly (Waks, 2007).

Developing countries like India are yet to make significant efforts towards adoption of online instruction to supplement traditional classroom teaching. Traditional classroom lectures continue to be the main mode of delivery of the core curriculum to undergraduate students in all Delhi University colleges, despite evidence that students' attention declines significantly and steadily after the first ten minutes of a lecture. In traditional classrooms, the learning process is passive. Studies have shown that active learning methods can enhance participation by the students, increase students' engagement with the course content and make the learning process more enriching.

This case focuses on the training of teachers on aspects of active and collaborative learning, aimed at increasing student participation. The objective was to familiarize the teachers in the use of Open Education Resources (OER). The authors also explored the concerns faced by the faculty members in adopting e-learning technologies. The case focuses on Delhi University, however the research questions and findings are equally relevant for other universities in India as well, wherever the main mode of teaching is on-campus and face-to-face.

Active and collaborative learning encourages innovation in both teaching and student involvement. Simple e-learning tools can be easily incorporated by students and / or professors. The use of a tool like Google Docs, for example, has enabled faculty and students to collaborate more efficiently and effectively on papers and presentations. Several of these innovative e-learning technologies such as Google Docs are available free of cost, or are very nominally priced. There is a gamut of such web 2.0 tools available on the Internet that may be used in the learning process. These tools encourage the students to build knowledge from multiple perspectives.

Status of E-Learning in Indian Universities – A Look at University of Delhi

Governments across the world are aware of the urgent need to educate adults who are not served by the existing institutions (HCPAC, 2009). E-learning and online education can play an important role in this context (Light, 2010). A number of countries have developed national e-learning strategies for the higher education sector.

India accounts for a quarter of the developing world's population and has one of the world's largest systems of higher education. With 221 Central and State Universities, 39 Deemed Universities and seven Open Universities in India (Kaul, 2006), the growth of higher education in India has been phenomenal. About 12 million students study in these universities and an additional 10 million study in over 6,500 vocational institutions.

The Government of India has been increasingly aware of the need for changes in the system of higher education in terms of use of new education technology (Light, Kanwar, Uvalic-Trumbic, 2009). It set up a "National Mission in Education through ICT" under its Eleventh Five–Year Plan (2007–2012) in order to promote the use of ICTs in education. To promote e-Learning, the country launched a dedicated satellite EDUSAT in 2004. Numerous e-Learning projects like eGyanKosh, Flexilearn, NPTEL, CEC, Institute of Lifelong Learning (ILLL), e-PG Pathshala have been launched to promote virtual learning environment (Thakur, 2013).

Delhi University Innovation Project

The University of Delhi (D.U.) is a Central University located in Delhi, India. It is a premier institute of higher education in India that is wholly funded by the Government of India. It offers courses at undergraduate and postgraduate levels. DU is one of the largest universities in India.

As the means and mode of education evolve, teachers and professors must also keep pace with technological developments. Often there is a lack of awareness amongst the faculty members about the opportunities for collaboration, learner participation and new types of interactive learning activities that are possible using e-learning tools. Research shows that active learning methods like collaborative learning can enhance active participation by the students, enrich student engagement with the course content and make the learning process more enriching. Active and collaborative learning increases student retention and limits anxiety. Students are not overloaded with information and it gives opportunities to connect the content to real life thus increasing learning. It also provides opportunities for higher order thinking as opposed to passive listening.

Delhi University Innovation Project was carried out by the team of teachers and students from Kamala Nehru College, University of Delhi in order to promote student participation and collaborative learning. The teacher training workshops were conducted in various colleges with the aim of making the faculty members aware of the e-learning applications that can help to promote active learning. Another objective was to assess the attitudes and receptiveness of faculty members towards adoption of such methods in their teaching.

CASE DISCUSSION

Motivation of the Project - Open Educational Resources (OERs)

One of the main objectives of the project was to make the faculty members aware of Open Education Resources. OERs refer to educational materials that are in the public domain, or introduced with an open license. Anyone can legally and freely copy, use, adapt and re-share them without "reinventing the wheel". OERs range from textbooks to curricula, syllabi, lecture notes, assignments, tests, projects, references and readings, simulations, experiments and demonstrations; and can be in the form of audio, video and animation.

In 2002, UNESCO held a forum comprising of some of the many people who wished to develop together a universal educational resource available for the whole of humanity. They described their efforts as the term "open educational resource". There are numerous active OER initiatives at colleges and universities around the world. Altogether, currently there are over 2000 freely available university courses online.

When using content that one did not create, it is important to make sure that copyright is not being violated. Work in public domain may be used freely without obtaining permission of former copyright owners. Creative Commons licensed content can also be used. OER can be found and used from Creative Commons materials, OER repositories and portals, websites or specialist repositories for research, learning and teaching resources. Creative commons licenses exist in a variety of combinations. These are given in Exhibit 1.

Exhibit 1: Combinations of Creative Commons Licenses

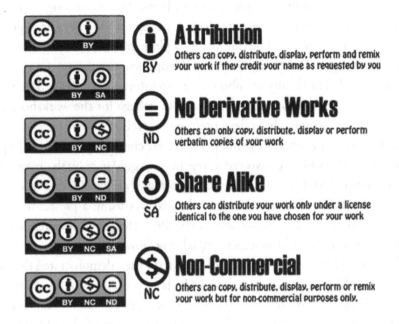

Source: http://research.gfcmsu.edu

Implementation of the Project

To attract the participants to the workshop, the subject chosen was "eCognitio: An Innovative E-learning Workshop Promoting Student Participation and Collaborative Learning."

Several colleges including Lady Shri Ram College, Deshbandhu College, College of Business studies, Shaheed Bhagat Singh College, Dyal Singh College etc. were approached with the proposal for holding the workshop in their colleges. In these colleges permission was taken from the head of the institution to verify that the selected colleges had a computer lab with adequate number of desktops and a reliable internet connection. The objective of the innovation project was described to the heads of the shortlisted colleges. For this pilot study, the aim was to get participation by faculty members from at least 15-20 colleges in Delhi.

The second year students of Kamala Nehru College were a part of the project, and were selected after a rigorous screening to assess their positive attitudes, ICT skills, intelligence and enthusiasm for the project. Initial training was provided to these students by the Principal Investigator so that they could assist faculties during the workshops. These day-long, hands-on faculty training workshops were conducted mostly on Saturdays or as per the convenience of the college. The training took place in the computer lab of these colleges as that gave the faculty members the opportunity to practice the tools being discussed. The faculty members were also informed beforehand that they need to carry their own computing devices to college for the workshop. The faculty could practice in the college premises, as well at home.

Skilled and experienced resource persons were chosen and invited to impart the training. The training involved a step-by-step guidance by the instructor. Instruction was first delivered in the lecture format with the aid of a PowerPoint presentation (PPT) that was shown to the learners using a projector. A few video tutorials were also embedded in the PPT that demonstrated various innovative e-learning technologies, explaining how they could be used for collaborative work by the learners. The instructor then demonstrated the steps to be followed live on the internet using the laptop that was plugged into the projector. Hand-outs of the slides of the PPT were given to all the teachers that would help them later when they practiced on their own, and enable them to recollect the process taught to them.

Participation in the Workshops

The participation in the workshop was extremely enthusiastic. The sessions were highly interactive. Apart from the hands-on training, the instructors motivated the participants and shared new-age teaching methods. They discussed the concept of flipped classroom and the techniques to incorporate it in classrooms. They shared that by utilizing these techniques, class time could be optimized, and the learning process made more enriching for the students. It would also make the task of imparting knowledge more exciting for the teachers.

The revolutionary concept of Massive Open Online Course (MOOC) was also discussed. The teachers were shown how they could create their own website without any cost using Google Sites. The feedback obtained from the participants at the end of the workshops in the form of discussions reinforced the perceived need for faculty training and development programs on a continuous basis.

Media Coverage

The project has been well covered in the media. It has been reported in Hindustan Times and the online editions of various newspapers.

FINDINGS OF THE STUDY

To analyse the attitudes of the faculty members towards e-learning mixed methods research was used (Tashakkori and Teddlie, 2003; McLeod 2008). The pre-workshop survey instrument was designed and developed in a systematic and structured manner. Considerable pilot work was done for the generation of items during questionnaire development in order to refine the wording and content. Exhibit 2 shows the questionnaire.

Exhibit 2: Collaborative Learning Workshop (Pre-workshop survey questionnaire)

Collaborative Learning Workshop (Faculty Development Program, KNC, DU, 23rd May 2016)
Pre-Workshop Survey

PROFESSION:_____ DATE: _____
INSTITUTION:_____

Q1. Have you heard of Collaborative Learning?
() Yes
() No

Q2. Are you familiar with the concept of a flipped classroom?
() Yes
() No

Q3. Are you familiar with any e-learning tools?
() Yes
() No

Q4. Please answer the frequency with which you use the following e-learning sources, tools and technologies.

Never	Rarely	Yearly	Monthly	Weekly	Daily
1	2	3	4	5	6

	Statement	
1	Computer	
2	Internet	
3	Email	
4	Word processing program such as Word	
5	Spreadsheet program such as Excel	
6	Presentation programs such as Power Point	
7	Social networking (Facebook, LinkedIn, Twitter)	
8	Web Conferencing (Skype, Google Chat)	
9	Media sharing sites (YouTube, Flickr)	
10	Smart phone (Blackberry, iPhone, Android)	
11	Learning Management System like Moodle or any other _____	
12	Collaboration tools (blogs, wikis, Google docs, Google Drive)	
13	Statistical software like SPSS, R, Minitab	
14	MOOCs	
15	Open Education Resources (OER)	
16	Paid Scholastic Sites like Jestor or other Digital Libraries	

Q5. Are you familiar with Open Education Resources?

() Yes

() No

IF YES, Please list the sources of OER's that you are aware of

_____

_____

_____

Q6. Do you know how to source videos and edit them as per needs of teaching and research?

() Yes () No

Q7. Please indicate if you agree or not with the following about the use of ICT in teaching.

Statement	Strongly Agree	Agree	Unde-cided	Strongly Disagree	Dis-agree
It is important to integrate information and communication technologies with traditional teaching methods.					
I select and use appropriate technologies that are particularly suited to my course learning outcomes.					
The use of ICT tools and e-learning methods in my courses increases student achievement and retention.					
I use little or no technology in my course, but wish to in the future.					
Technology isn't particularly valuable in teaching my discipline.					
I would like to use e-learning tools more effectively in my teaching.					
I generally do NOT need assistance or support when using new technologies.					
I am generally uncomfortable with new technologies.					
I do not know how to incorporate e-learning methods in my course(s).					

Q8. Do you think that Collaborative learning is an effective way of learning for the students?

() Yes () No

IF YES, how feasible do you think it is in the context of your college and university with the given resources and set up? (Rate from 0 to 10) _____

Q9. What pedagogical tools would you like to learn to enhance your teaching?

_____

_____

_____

_____

Q10. What part of the courses you take in your college emphasises collaborative learning?

_____

_____

_____

_____

Q11. Do you have resource persons on your campus to ask for help with technological problems and challenges?

() Yes () No

Q12. Anything else that you would like to share with us before the workshop:

_____

It was an anonymous survey. Four questions in the questionnaire are qualitative in nature and eight are quantitative. The questionnaire was administered at the end of the workshop.

Key highlights of the survey have been presented:

1. Awareness of Types of OER among participants

The faculty members mostly referred to e-library, e-books, e-pathshala, online journals, Jstor, wikieducator, online videos and Google. The responses showed that though the faculty members may have heard of OER, most of them did not have a very accurate idea of what it was. There were very few (about 10%) who answered that they were aware of OER and mentioned accurate sources like MIT Open Courseware, university websites and government websites.

2. E-learning tools that participants are eager to learn

There were varied answers like e-books, animation, videos, how to make animated presentations, ways of using OER, and new ways to collaborate. Many of the teachers also expressed the desire to learn very basic things like how to make PPTs. Phrases like "wish to enrich our teaching method using technology" and "enhance classroom teaching" were used. Respondents also expressed interest to know more about MOOCs, blogs, wikis, Google Docs and Google Drive.

3. Courses in college that emphasized on collaborative learning

Participants mentioned projects and practical courses. Some emphasized that the interaction with students in the classroom in the form of discussions was also collaborative in nature. Practical subjects like GIS, remote sensing, projects on Indian Economy, Botany theory and bio-informatics practical were also mentioned.

4. Other general comments

This drew a variety of responses like:

- "I am keen to integrate technology in teaching".
- "Such workshops are very beneficial for teaching."
- "Good effort to increase communication between teachers who wish to learn new ways of teaching."
- "E-learning needs to be encouraged and adopted widely, but internet connectivity remains a hurdle in many contexts."
- "Validation of online content is important."
- "Information should be oriented towards hands-on practical training."
- "Want to learn how to use e-resources and to make teaching more interesting and informative."
- "E-learning still faces many infrastructural hurdles in a college like ours but once it is done, the results are wonderful."

Overall, the qualitative research questions showed the interest levels were high among the participants for learning e-learning applications. This was subsequently reflected when they enthusiastically participated in the discussions on the constraints faced by teachers in various colleges, and the efforts to overcome them. The teachers were also excited to learn the hands-on component of the workshop in which they were shown how to create a Google Site of their own that could be used to create a flipped classroom.

By analysing the responses of the quantitative questions several interesting conclusions were derived:

- When asked if they had heard of collaborative learning, 78.2% of the respondents said yes and only 21.8% said no.
- However, only 23.8% of the teachers expressed familiarity with concept of flipped learning.
- 54.1% of the professors said that they were not familiar with any e-learning tools.
- 60.9% of the participants expressed lack of knowledge of the concept of Open Education Resources.
- Only 28.2% of the participants said that they knew how to source videos and how to edit them.
- When asked if the thought that collaborative learning was an effective way of learning for students, 86.7% of them answered in the affirmative.
- In a crucial question, the faculty members were asked if they had any resource person on their campus to ask for help with technological problems and challenges. While 52.4% said no, 47.6% said that they did have such person(s).

Exhibit 2 gives the frequency of use of e-learning sources, tools and technologies. The questionnaire asked the respondents if they agreed or not with the certain statements about the use of ICT in teaching. The preliminary data analysis yielded the results as shown in Exhibit 3.

Exhibit 2: Frequency of Use of E-Learning Sources

S. No.	Frequency of use of technology	Never	Rarely	Yearly	Monthly	Weekly	Daily
1	Computer	0 (0%)	8 (6.8%)	0 (0%)	0 (0%)	19 (16.15%)	91 (77.35%)
2	Internet	0 (0%)	10 (8.5%)	0 (0%)	0 (0%)	10 (8.5%)	88 (74.8%)
3	Email	0 (0%)	10 (8.5%)	0 (0%)	0 (0%)	28 (23.8%)	80 (68%)
4	Word processing program like MS Word	0 (0%)	12 (10.2%)	0 (0%)	8 (6.8%)	46 (39.1%)	52 (44.2%)
5	Spreadsheet program like MS Excel	0 (0%)	18 (15.3%)	0 (0%)	114 (96.9%)	36 (30.6%)	20 (17%)
6	Presentation program like PowerPoint	0 (0%)	8 (6.8%)	0 (0%)	44 (37.4%)	52 (44.2%)	14 (11.9%)
7	Social networking (Facebook, LinkedIn, Twitter)	6 (5.1%)	24 (20.4%)	0 (0%)	11 (9.35%)	19 (16.15%)	58 (49.3%)
8	Web conferencing (Skype, Google Chat)	16 (13.6%)	18 (15.3%)	4 (3.4%)	6 (5.1%)	43 (36.55%)	31 (26.35%)
9	Media sharing sites (YouTube, Flickr)	12 (10.2%)	8 (6.8%)	4 (3.4%)	20 (17%)	30 (25.5%)	44 (37.4%)
10	Smart phone	8 (6.8%)	4 (3.4%)	0 (0%)	4 (3.4%)	8 (6.8%)	94 (79.9%)
11	Learning management system like Moodle or any other	52 (44.2%)	50 (42.5%)	0 (0%)	4 (3.4%)	8 (6.8%)	4 (3.4%)
12	Collaboration tools (Blogs, Wikis, Google Docs, Google Drive)	30 (25.5%)	27 (22.95%)	4 (3.4%)	21 (17.85%)	27 (22.95%)	9 (7.65%)
13	Statistical Software like SPSS, R, Minitab	41 (34.85%)	25 (21.25%)	14 (11.9%)	25 (21.25%)	13 (11.05%)	0 (0%)
14	MOOCs	66 (56.1%)	27 (22.95%)	7 (5.95%)	8 (6.8%)	4 (3.4%)	8 (6.8%)
15	Open Education Resources (OER)	46 (39.1%)	23 (19.55%)	16 (13.6%)	21 (17.85%)	3 (2.55%)	9 (7.65%)
16	Paid scholastic sites like Jstor or other Digital Libraries	59 (50.15%)	15 (12.75%)	4 (3.4%)	25 (21.25%)	11 (9.35%)	4 (3.4%)

Source: Authors

Exhibit 3: Responses for Use of ICT in Teaching

Statement	Strongly disagree	Disagree	Undecided	Agree	Strongly agree
It is important to integrate ICT with traditional teaching methods	0%	0%	0%	50 (42.37%)	68 (57.8)
I select and use appropriate technologies that are particularly suited to my course	0%	0%	16 (13.6%)	54 (45.9%)	48 (40.8%)
The use of e-learning methods in my courses increases student achievement and attention	0%	0%	12 (10.2%)	53 (40.1%)	53 (40.1%)
I use little or no technology in my course but wish to in the future.	20 (17%)	28 (23.8%)	22 (18.7%)	34 (28.9%)	14 (11.9%)
Technology is not of particular value in teaching in my discipline	49 (41.7%)	49 (41.7%)	12 (10.2%)	4 (3.4%)	4 (3.4%)
I would like to use e-learning tools more effectively in my teaching	0%	8 (6.8%)	4 (3.4%)	48 (40.8%)	58 (49.3%)
I generally do not need assistance or support when using new technologies	23 (19.55%)	49 (41.7%)	18 (15.3%)	24 (20.4%)	4 (3.4%)
I am generally uncomfortable with new technologies	30 (25.5%)	46 (39.1%)	14 (11.9%)	20 (17%)	8 (6.8%)
I do not know how to incorporate e-learning methods in my course(s)	22 (18.7%)	26 (22.1%)	10 (8.5%)	34 (28.9%)	6 (5.1%)

Source: Authors

CONCLUSION

Barriers to Faculty Acceptance of E-Learning Applications

During the past decade, there has been a significant movement toward blended formats of learning where traditional classroom instruction is combined with online interaction. Research has also clearly supported the implementation of blended teaching in college courses (Ocak, 2010). Yet the most commonly cited factor inhibiting the development of online degree programs is faculty acceptance of online education (Stewart et al., 2010). Studies have shown that approximately 95% of faculty members continue to believe that traditional lecture is the most effective means to achieve student learning outcomes (Yang & Cornelious, 2005). Identifying factors that lead to faculty acceptance of online education are of central importance to achieve the goals of universities to integrate technology in education (Stewart et al., 2010). Faculty development programs often overlook factors that promote or inhibit the use of technologies among professors (Marshall 2011, Stacey & Gerbic, 2008). One of the objectives of this study was to identify the factors that encourage or pose hurdles to the use of e-learning to supplement their classroom instruction for the academic staff of Delhi University.

REFERENCES

Kaul, S. (2006). Higher Education in India: Seizing the Opportunity. *The Indian Council for Research on International.* Working Paper No. 179. Retrieved October 13, 2016, from http://www.icrier.org/pdf/WP_179.pdf

Light, D. (2010). Multiple Factors Supporting the Transition to ICT-Rich Learning Environments. *International Journal of Education and Development Using Information and Communication Technology,* 6(4), 39–51.

Marshall, S. (2011). Change, Technology and Higher Education: Are Universities Capable of Organizational Change? ALT-J, Research in Learning Technology, 18(3), 179–192.

McLeod, S. (1970). Qualitative vs. Quantitative. Retrieved October 14, 2016, from http://www.simplypsychology.org/qualitative-quantitative.html

Ocak, M. A. (2010). World Journal on Educational Blend or Not to Blend: A Study Investigating Faculty Members Perceptions of Blended Teaching. *World Journal on Educational Technology,* 2(3), 196–210.

Stacey, E. & Gerbic, P. (2008). Success Factors for Blended Learning. In Hello! Where are you in the Landscape of Educational Technology?, *Proceedings of Ascilite Melbourne 2008.* Retrieved October 3, 2016, from http://www.ascilite.org.au/conferences/melbourne08/procs/stacey.pdf

Stewart, C., Bachman, C., & Johnson, R. (2010). Predictors of Faculty Acceptance of Online Education. *MER Journal of Online Learning and*

Teaching, 6(3), 597–616. Retrieved September 4, 2016 from http://jolt. merlot.org/vol6no3/stewartc_0910.pdf

Tashakkori, A., and Teddlie, C. (1998). *Mixed Methodology: Combining Qualitative and Quantitative Approaches*. Thousand Oaks, CA: Sage Publications.

Thakur, A. (2013). E-Learning: Initiatives in India. *Open Journal of Education*, 1(2), 61.

Toth, K. (2011). An Organizational Approach for Sustaining E-Learning in a Large Urban University. *In International Conference - The Future of Education*. Retrieved Ocotber 15, 2016, from http://conference.pixelonline. net/edu_future/common/download/Paper_pdf/ELE22-Toth.pdf

Yang, Y., & Cornelius, L. F. (2005). Preparing instructors for quality online instruction. *Online Journal of Distance Learning Administration*, 8, 12-31. Retrieved October 20, 2016, from http://www.westga.edu/~distance/ojdla/ spring81/yang81.htm

Waks, L. (2007). The Concept of Fundamental Educational Change. *Educational Theory*, 57(3), 277–96.

SECTION

HUMAN RESOURCES

A Story Of A Banker - Corporate Mergers & Acquisitions And Its Impact On Human Resources

Author Bio

Dr. Narinder Bhasin

Dr. Bhasin is a distinguished senior banking professional and research scholar with 31 years in the banking industry and academic experience as visiting / adjunct faculty. He is pursuing his second Ph.D. from Amity University. He is a qualified CAIIB, MBA and Certified Bank Trainer with expertise in establishing and restructuring banking systems and processes, objectives and goals.

He has worked in foreign banks like ANZ Grindlays and Standard Chartered as well as private sector banks like ING Vysya Bank and HDFC Bank Ltd. His last assignment was as Vice President, Axis Bank. He is presently working as a Professor in Amity School of Insurance, Banking and Actuarial Science (ASIBAS) at Amity University, Noida, Uttar Pradesh.

He was a part of Reserve Bank of India as member of Reconciliation Group and Working Group for settlement of clearing disputes and writing procedural guidelines of Cheque Truncation System respectively. He has been an eminent speaker, panelist and presenter at reputed national and international conferences, seminars and forums. He has also authored multiple publications related to the BFSI industry. He is also a fellow member of Indian Institute of Banking and Finance.

EXECUTIVE SUMMARY

Mergers and acquisitions (M&A) is not a new concept. There have been numerous cases of two companies coming together and joining hands. The end goal can be to consolidate and become a market leader, improve efficiency of operations, integrate business, aid in business expansion etc. The main reasons of a recent increase in number of M&As in India and around the globe can be attributed to globalization, computerization, accelerated growth, vertical integration, diversification, seeking tax advantage and technological improvements. This case is a reflection of perception of M&A on the human resources and employees of the merged companies. Various synergies like operating, financial, managerial and sales are considered. These synergies allow for additional benefits that can be derived from resources of two companies. The most important motive and synergy which is either forgotten or given a back seat is Human Resources Synergy which is imperative for converting the vision of M&A through Economic Value Added and Market Value Added methods. The case study assesses the post-merger impact on human resources and why people leave organizations and / or feel dissatisfied. For every eight failures, there is a case where both companies emerge stronger (such as the merger between Fiat and Chrysler after the latter emerged from filing for bankruptcy). In most cases, success can be achieved when people in both organization show that they value each other, and actively work together.

SETTING THE STAGE

After fifteen years of my work experience managing big teams, I realize the true concept of management with human values. I realize that while they are called professionals, many organizations are treating their employees as resources, like other fixed assets. When the fixed assets depreciate after constant use, they are written off or disposed. The organizations care for output without focusing on human needs and values. Though the organizations do not focus on professional development, when they find that these employees have grown old and are not updated with the latest information and techniques, they wish to throw them out and recruit young people. Employees who have devoted their lives to work and success of organization are bewildered when they are asked to leave suddenly.

Change is imperative to achieve repeated success in organizations, irrespective of the sector. Rapidly changing technology, and frequent changes in Internet and mobile communications has changed the way businesses function. Due to the fast changing needs of customers, organizations are striving to keep pace and evolve rapidly to manufacture products or provide services to achieve customer satisfaction and delight.

Marketing of products and services in the digital world is the key to success. Regulations and compliance issues hold immense importance. This case represents the merger of two large foreign banks operating in India which was undertaken due to non-regulatory compliance of banking process by top management. It is discussed how the staff of merged banks had to face difficulties involving attrition, dissatisfaction, mental harassment and loss of pride.

Analysis and subsequent findings from the case show that the best way of handling this entire journey of a merger should be handled by the Human Resource department with more care. They should provide extensive counseling services to the staff, especially to the employees who are losing their job after 30-40 years of service.

Another observation is that at times despite adequate care being taken by organizations involving cognizance of the intricacies, the M&A process fails due to shortfalls in the integration or transition process. The press release announcing any new merger or acquisition is always quick to announce the benefit to the consumer first, the shareholders, and the principals (CEOs, investment bankers, lawyers), but usually lacks the employee perspective.

ORGANIZATION BACKGROUND

The NBI Bank of India was formed in 1863 and became one of the largest overseas banks based out of London, operating not only in the Indian sub-continent but in countries around the Indian Ocean. In 1948 it purchased the smaller ND Bank, London, renaming itself GND Bank some ten years later. Following further acquisitions in 1974, GND was taken over by A2Z Group in 1984 and renamed A2Z Bank.

STC Bank was formed in 1969 through the merger of two separate banks, the Sophia Bank of British South Africa and the Trans Bank of India, Australia and China. These banks had capitalised on the expansion of trade between

Europe, Asia and Africa. STC Bank acquired A2Z Bank in 2000. After the merger the A2Z name fell out of use.

Merger of A2Z Bank with STC Bank

In July 2001 the merger took place. The newly merged entity was able to achieve significant synergies through operating efficiencies and revenue enhancements. The deal added to the strength of STC Bank management resources and helped it become India's leading bank. It also helped create a premier international banking business in Middle East and Asia, thus emerging as a leading consumer bank in the region. With the successful merger of A2Z Bank to its fold, STC Bank's total assets touched USD 5 billion, making it the largest foreign bank in the country. Mr. JSB, STC CEO, Indian operations said in a statement, "The Indian operations of A2Z have merged with STC Bank as on August 31, 2002 and the bank is happy to announce that all aspects of this exercise have been successfully accomplished and with a formal approval from the Reserve Bank."

He also stated, "The significant value that the A2Z franchise has brought to the STC Banking group was clearly reflected in their annual results for 2001-02 and India is now a key market for growth within the group." He said the merger would put them in a position to deliver significant benefits in terms of network, products and customer service. The bank planned to open branches in Chandigarh, Ludhiana, Lucknow and Jaipur by the end of the calendar year and plans were afoot to expand distribution in the current cities of operation.

The bank had presence in 15 cities across the country. In June, A2Z Bank and STC together recorded USD 140 million operating profit.

Human Resource Strategies Adopted by STC Bank

Benefits derived from the merger and the subsequent synergies of the combined entity resulted in a positive post-merger performance. Unfortunately, there was a major fallout of the merger in the form of voluntary retirements (VRS), forced retirements, and lowering of retirement age from 60 to 55. For the existing staff members, interviews were held which would determine their continuance in the organization. The top management also decided to upgrade the clerical staff by offering them managerial cadres for clerical duties.

Clerical staff was offered waiver of loans whereas management staff that the organisation wished to terminate were labelled as non-performers and were asked to leave.

CASE DESCRIPTION

It was September 2001. I was called by my boss and informed that I have been nominated from Northern India for banking operations on-the-job training at the Fort Mumbai Branch. He also advised that I have to leave immediately the next morning. When I asked the agenda for the training programme, he told me that I will be informed at the venue. In the past when I had imparted training the agenda, content and modules were prepared in advance. I was therefore concerned and had doubts in my mind due to the mode in which I was informed about this training programme and the rapid manner in which it happened. My concerns proved to be correct as the next day when I reached the venue at Mumbai, it was advised that forced voluntary retirement (VRS) has been planned for the senior staff in clerical cadre with few incentives. It was instructed to transfer the senior staff to a newly created Resource Management Cell (RMC) department. It was planned that these employees will be made to sit idle and no fresh work will be allotted. A team of four members, including me, were asked to train and impart on-the-job training to freshers with graduate degrees who were recruited at a low salary of USD 100.

It was a great setback for me. It distressed me when I realized that employees who have served these organizations diligently for years are being treated as unusable, adversely impacting their regular income, which they needed for family obligations and other commitments. The same day, in the evening several staff members came to my room seeking clarity on their future. Their entire financial planning was affected and they were troubled. I did not have any answer for their queries, except to console them and give them hope to face these bad times with courage, and assuring them that things will settle soon.

These staff members left my room but that whole night I could not sleep. My conscience was not ready to accept the fact that the top management could be so apathetic towards staff needs and their problems. I realized that they are using us to train these young people, but once they are trained and able to manage the work themselves, we will also not be required. I further examined that these people have been so sincere in their 25 - 35 years of work experience but they have neither tried to update themselves with the outside world in banking industry, nor academically updated themselves. No manager and team leader had taken any initiative to develop and nurture their talent.

Early morning the next day I woke up feeling fresher, and committed to improve the state of affairs. I realized that my team members need to constantly learn, share their knowledge, and develop their skills so that they become multi-talented. I could not do much for these employees at that moment as I was also a part of management forced to take VRS at that stage, but this merger gave me some food for thought and made me more insightful. My concerns were proved to be correct. After clerical cadre, managerial staff was also forced to retire or opt for VRS. The same process was repeated later in Delhi and other centres also.

CASE DISCUSSION

With this realization of human values for caring for my team, updating and developing professionally as well as personally; my vision for leadership and mentorship underwent a drastic shift with human values as the top priority. I adopted a 24/7/365 approach to leadership rather one based on a 10am to 5pm schedule. I started interacting frequently and more intimately with my team members, attempting to genuinely understand their personal, career and social goals. In addition to playing the role of a manager and a leader, I also started assisting them with activities aimed at their holistic improvement. I started enhancing their conversational skills, and focused on training and development. Despite personality development of my team members not being assigned as my KRA (Key Responsibility Area), I considered it as a part of my human values vision. Irrespective of designations, whether it is an outsourced person or a permanent employee, I started interacting with them and convinced them to enhance their skills by acquiring new certifications. I was proven successful as my attempts empowered them to attain rapid professional growth in the organization. I motivated and encouraged highly-talented people to take up better opportunities when I realized that our organization would not be able to promote them or give incentives commensurate with their potential, due to the constraints in their Human Resource policies.

Over the years I have helped several people plan their personal goals and careers. With them my relations transcend a mere manager-employee relationship. I cherish the opportunity and platform that I had to administer a method of leadership and management based on human values in a more effective manner.

With this paradigm shift in my thinking, my philosophy for management based on human values also underwent drastic change. The mission of my life is "Let's learn, teach, share and develop". While handling big teams and imparting on-the-job training, I came in touch with various business schools where I had an opportunity to share my experiences and thoughts, write articles and papers on various topics of banking, finance, and economics. I re-joined IIBF and qualified two certificate courses on AML / KYC and Trade Finance. I also completed an Indian Bank Association research on Impact of Technology on payment systems and was awarded with an award and scholarship. All these efforts were directed not for any self-achievement and appreciation, but as an enabler for me to share my vision with my students and disciples, which is to develop their academic and technical skills.

The most important lesson learnt is that every individual must enhance his market value by creating his second or third backup of source of earning by equipping themselves with higher education as well as business skills.

EPILOGUE

The name of A2Z was removed and it became STC Bank. For the world it was a merger but employees considered it as an acquisition. In 2003, I also resigned from STC Bank though I was elevated to the post of a Manager in December 2002. I was keen to work with an organisation that cares for human values and treats its employee not merely as a resource but as equal opportunity partners. I joined and was elevated to senior positions in two large Indian private sector banks – HCF Bank and ABC Bank, and worked for twelve years in the senior position of Vice President.

With my experience I realize that business is only driven my virtue of monetary success, and there is a dearth of human values, emotions, and mentoring future professional leaders. Marketing oneself is of paramount importance while ethics and compliance takes a backseat.

Employees need opportunities for growth. Organizations should ensure this through training and development, promotions and job rotation. Additionally, employees contribute to the success of organizations not merely by virtue of their KRA but also act as partners. Therefore, implications for employees should be considered carefully during important decisions like M&As. Human values should be kept in mind during M&As, and even if it imperative to let go of an employee, it should be done as a friendly exit, ensuring that the employee needs are taken care of.

CONCLUSION

- One size does not fit all. Many companies feel that the best way to get ahead is to expand ownership boundaries through M&As. For others separating the public ownership of a subsidiary or business segment offers more advantages.
- Mergers create synergies, economies of scale, helps in expanding operations, and helps cut costs.
- M&As come in all shapes and sizes. Investors need to consider the complex issues involved in M&As.
- The most beneficial form of equity structure involves a complete analysis of the costs and benefits associated with the deals.
- Role of Human Resource is extremely important. They need to take all the staff members in confidence during M&As.
- Each and every individual must keep on learning both academically as well as professionally.

Inexperienced But Overqualified Employees: The Human Resource Perspective

Author Bio

Gargi Singh

Gargi is currently pursuing Ph.D. in Management from Amity Business School, Amity University. She has done her graduation in Mechanical Engineering from G.B. Pant Engineering College affiliated to H.N.B Garhwal University and MS in Human Resource Management from ICFAI University. She has an interest in the field of psychology has completed her M.A. in Psychology, with Clinical Psychology as her major. Her experience encompasses varied fields and organizations during her study tenure. She is pursuing her Ph.D. in the field of Stress Management.

EXECUTIVE SUMMARY

The case study discusses scenarios faced by Human Resources in handling overqualified but inexperienced employees. Overqualification is considered a multidimensional term, and is one of various types of insufficient employment. It is a condition where the employment is of minor quality in comparison to the job standard. Overqualification is an enormous reason for dissatisfaction. As per several studies overqualification plays a significant role in employee dissatisfaction resulting in low or counter productivity, burnout, or employee leaving jobs. The problem becomes more complicated when handling employees who are overqualified, but have limited experience. The case study deals with understanding problems with such employees and presents a Human Resource perspective.

SETTING THE STAGE

Arvind has an MBA degree in Finance. He had been unemployed after completing his education. He started searching for a job immediately after completion of his education, as being the eldest amongst four siblings, he realized he has a lot of responsibilities towards his family. Arvind's father, Mr. Kukreja, an ex-government employee, retired two years ago. Since his retirement the family had been in a financial crisis. Arvind has two younger brothers and a younger sister in his family. All three are still in college and are therefore dependent on the family for support. When Arvind's father Mr. Kukreja was working, there was no financial burden on Arvind, but post his retirement, several monetary issues emerged. The family responsibility fell on Arvind and it was important for him to solve these financial problems. Arvind was a bright student in his school and college life, and therefore had high aspirations. He wished to wait and search for a management position in the finance department of a large company, but eventually decided to start applying for jobs which were not matching his profile and ability.

Overqualification is considered as a multidimensional term, and is one of various types of insufficient employment. It is a condition where the employment is of minor quality in comparison to the job standard. Overqualification can arise due to two major factors: over-experience; or mismatch of skills with job, education, or experience.

General perception is that these candidates do not possess necessary skills to get a job. Studies show that personnel managers prefer to hire those applicants who adequately qualify for the job, rather than those overqualified or underqualified. The theoretical basis behind selecting the overqualified persons can be aligned to the idea of individual job fit – which states that a candidate's ability should be matched by requirements of the job.

CASE DISCUSSION

Last year, Anubha, a Senior Managing Director at Finance Direct needed to hire a finance executive for their company, which was a small but growing global non-for-profit financial organization. She assumed that the best candidate would be somebody comparatively young but with a few years of non-profit finance area experience. She was not expecting an inexperienced candidate like Arvind. Arvind had almost no industry experience other than some basic training during his internship. During the training period, he had spent time in the metal industry in the role of a management trainee. He did not have any experience of working with a non-profit organization or social enterprise. He also did not have any experience of finance industry, but he did possess a thorough understanding of finance domain, and was deeply enthusiastic to work in financial companies.

This was not an unfamiliar situation for Finance Direct. They frequently received resumes of candidates who were inexperienced, despite the job post clearly stating that they required a few years of work experience. These candidates typically had a lot of enthusiasm, but lacked experience of working in the finance sector. Anubha had earlier ruled out applicants who did not possess relevant experience or who were overqualified for certain positions.

Arvind came with a strong recommendation letter from his college, and Anubha thought that his understanding of finance domain and enthusiasm might help Finance Direct deal with problems faced by financial department of large MNC's. She discussed this with Human Resource department, and they all agreed that there were inherent risks with employing Arvind as he had never worked in the sector. But they saw many positives too. "We did not have anyone on our staff who was so young. We knew that he would enable us to come up with unhindered and fresh ideas, working with passion and diligence," explained Human Resource. They analysed in detail the risks and opportunities of hiring him, as he was overqualified for the job, and at the same time inexperienced.

1. Opportunities

- Will learn and adapt quickly.
- Will help others develop skills.
- Will be a bargain in terms of hiring costs.
- Will serve as a mascot for future prospective candidates.
- Will work with much more dedication than older employees.

2. Risks

- Existing senior employees might not be happy.
- If under-utilized, will be a liability for the company.
- Work behaviour may be counterproductive for others.
- Productivity may be limited and learning curve steep.

After analyzing, Human Resource team concluded that the opportunities outweighed the risks. They had been overwhelmed with Arvind's willingness to learn what he did not know. "Hunger to learn and potential are the most important criteria we consider while hiring candidates," Anubha explained, "We look for potential, not necessarily for astuteness. We hire people who can thrive, gel, and evolve."

The Risk Pays Off

Arvind joined the company. Human Resource encouraged and helped him to network with finance managers from other companies, so that he could take advantage from the insights from experts in the domain of finance. They also provided him requisite training and on-field experience. The learning curve was steep but he was able to learn and grasp quickly, and is now flourishing in his role. Looking at his potential they are also looking forward to elevate him to a management position so that they can also leverage his higher degree for the job which made him overqualified initially.

As Finance Direct plans expansion into more sectors, they have been able to leverage directly into his management degree in finance. While Arvind did not fit the bill of the type of candidate Human Resource initially planned to hire, both the organization and Arvind had evolved together – and used his strengths and skills which benefitted them both.

While it may seem that for any sort of employment the right fit of education level is required, the rule may not hold true. This simple picture of relationship between work and education infers that where lower qualified workers are employed, the productivity will be zero. In contrast, people possessing higher qualification are considered to be underutilizing their abilities. Their efficiency in a position below their educational level equals the efficiency of employee with an ample educational background for this type of job. Job satisfaction could be defined as a feeling of positivism about one's work which results from an assessment of its characteristics.

Recent studies show that overqualification, when not associated with skill underutilization, is merely a minute issue for job contentment. When associated with skills underutilization, overqualification is a substantive issue.

Conclusion

Performance at workplace is assumed to be adversely impacted when the candidate is overqualified. This case shows that this may not always be the case. Studies typically shows that there is a universal practice of personnel managers rejecting job applicants with overqualification, as these applicants are more probable to form or develop negative attitudes towards their job, thus affecting their performance.

Moreover, there should be a practice employed by Human Resource to ensure that over qualified candidates are given opportunities to grow within an organization, so that their abilities and potential can be leveraged for the benefit of both the candidate as well as the organization.

Questions For Discussion

1. Is over qualification really a problem in every scenario?
2. If better growth environment is provided, can overqualified employees thrive as well?

3. How can organizations leverage overqualified employees and appropriately utilize the employee's skills benefiting both of them?

4. How can companies set expectations while hiring overqualified candidates?

MOBILES AT WORKPLACE: THE NEW AGE CHALLENGE

AUTHOR BIO

Geeta Kumar

Geeta Kumar is an Independent Organisational Development Consultant with over 23 years of experience in the areas of Human Resource and Organizational Development, having handled diverse and challenging assignments with Indian and overseas clients. Previously she has worked in the corporate sector with leading organizations such as NIIT, Eicher Motors, Times of India Group and CII.

She is trained in Process Work from Aastha, a national level not-for-profit educational institution that is dedicated to fostering of human processes - the key ingredient for Organisational Development and Personal Growth. A certified FIRO-B and MBTI practitioner, she holds double Masters, in Management and in Women and Gender Studies; and is also currently pursuing her Doctoral Research at Amity University.

She is also associated with Consumers India as a Mentor for their Internship Programmes which takes up studies and researches covering a gamut of important consumer issues.

Executive Summary

Mobile use is a necessity at the workplace. It provides a convergence of all media technologies rolled into one single device. While the consequences of mobile use are usually considered to be an enabler, inappropriate mobile use can have outcomes that create significant liabilities, both from an organizational as well as an individual perspective. Inappropriate mobile use at the workplace could include discourtesies such as loud talk, interruptions at meeting, viewing or sending inappropriate content, stealing organizational data and information, recording, misusing phone conversations, and sexual harassment issues.

Organizations have, to some extent, been able to contain misuse of official internet on personal laptops and computers by installing requisite software and firewalls, monitoring of employees, and formulating acceptable Internet policies. Technology changes rapidly though, and organizations need to become more proactive towards the realities of misuse of mobile at the workplace.

Utilizing SKS group as a backdrop, this case study explores the various dimensions of the issues of inappropriate mobile use at the workplace. The case reveals how a pro-active, participative and collaborative approach can contain and mitigate this issue. This is key since this process would instil a high level of responsible behaviour and would ensure higher adherence to formalized mobile ethics norms.

This case will be of immense value for organizations to understand the organizational and employee implications as well as the various dimensions of mobile use at the workplace. It would also serve as a guide to formalize effective and customized rules and policies towards mobile ethics at the workplace.

Setting The Stage

Vanshika, the Group Human Resource Head of a diversified Indian conglomerate based out of NCR, was suddenly perplexed by the forceful debate that emerged during their weekly departmental meeting on the need to formally establish mobile usage norms at the workplace. The immediate trigger were two instances within the group companies. In the first instance, an employee was confronted on being found to watch inappropriate content at his workstation. In the second instance, by recording a phone conversation of a colleague, it was found that an employee was compromising organizational information.

In both these instances there were no clear cut organizational policies and rules laid out regarding ethics on mobile phone usage at workplace, and the specific disciplinary action that should be initiated. This discussion raised some fundamental questions, such as:

- What constitutes inappropriate workplace mobile phone use?
- What is the extent of this menace?
- What are the consequences to the organization and the individual employee?
- What should be the ways to address the issue of mobile ethics at the workplace?

In order to find a way forward to tackle this issue, Vanshika decided to form a taskforce to study the issue of inappropriate mobile phone usage in depth and develop an implementation plan.

ORGANIZATIONAL BACKGROUND

SKS Group is a diversified Indian conglomerate employing over 2000 employees pan-India with an annual turnover of over USD 1 billion. Its businesses straddle Agri–Rural products, Industrial products, and high end building infrastructure. It has its factories in North and Western India and a pan-India sales and marketing. The group has well-defined processes in all its manufacturing facilities, and lays a high emphasis on continuous improvements and upgradation, in terms of both its employees and technologies. The organization is considered as being very proactive on its people processes, organizational culture, safety, and health & environment issues. The group is also considered as a Preferred Employer and a Great Workplace. The workforce is diversified and consists of semi educated workers to highly qualified professionals from premium educational institutions from India and abroad.

CASE DISCUSSION

Vanshika entrusted this study to a cross functional team of five members who formed a taskforce. This team was given the task to analyze the current scenario of mobile phone usage, and come out with recommendations.

The team initially conducted exploratory open-ended interviews among a cross section of employees both at the factories and at the corporate office. The objective was to understand the scope, meaning and dimensions of inappropriate mobile use at the workplace.

A total of 25 employees were interviewed over a period of 10 days. The team, to their surprise, found the issue complex and multi-dimensional. The issues that were discussed by the participating employees were wide-ranging, such as:

- Distractive tendency of mobile at workplace
- Doing personal work during work hours
- Viewing inappropriate content
- Sexual harassment
- Unauthorized copying of official and confidential organization information on the mobile
- Recording conversations without the knowledge of other party
- Need for mobile use courtesy and protocols, and self-discipline

Some examples of conversations have been shared:

Employee 1, Female, 37 years: "Office / Work WhatsApp groups lighten up the atmosphere, but can also be distractive. Inappropriate content being shared is also a concern. Many times information shared on these common platforms may not be relevant to everyone in the group, and ideally should be shared one-on-one. Personal opinions creep in and take away the objective and factual information sharing agenda of these groups"

Employee 2, Male, 42 years: "At work mobile can be misused for taking pictures without permission and for sending official data out of the organization without approval. In our organization, often people have been recording official conversations that gets used against the other party. This has led to people becoming more cautious of what they speak on their mobiles. Also there have been cases of sexual harassment of employees – such as inappropriate pictures and messages being sent on WhatsApp".

Employee 3, Female, 26 years: "People post inappropriate content and pictures on social media, not realizing the consequences at work or with clients. Information can be shared with the click of a button. People should use discretion. There are instances when employees record conversations implicating their bosses, or the other way round. These have been several occasions of breach of ethical issues that have not been formally dealt with".

Employee 4, Male, 51 years: "I usually keep my phone on vibration mode so that it does not disturb others. I believe that mobile etiquettes demand that the phone be picked up within a few rings or a quick message sent. This is basic courtesy and respect that is not displayed by people. Meetings get disturbed when someone's phone rings. Sensitization on mobile do's and don'ts is required especially in a work context. Our company has blocked usage of certain internet sites so they cannot be accessed even from the mobile. Despite this, the danger of sharing confidential documents on mobile exists and is a very real danger".

Employee 5, Male, 38 years: "Data Safety, inappropriate content, sexual harassment, and sting operations are dark realities due to mobile use at the workplace."

The interviews were very insightful since it made the taskforce aware of the nature and depth of the problem. They also revealed that there was an urgent need to address this issue real-time, and that the employees were open to a formalized set of norms to be put in place and implemented. Based on these interviews, and undertaking literature review on existing and current papers and articles, a detailed list of "Inappropriate Workplace Mobile Use" was compiled by the taskforce.

The taskforce then presented a preliminary roadmap to the Group Human Resource Head, Vanshika.

Being an employee-centric organization and possessing a high employee engagement orientation, the task force strongly believed that "the problems and solutions all lie within the organization".

Extending the adage of killing two birds with one stone, the taskforce suggested a three-pronged approach:

1. Capturing real time information on frequency and perception of inappropriate workplace mobile phone usage.

2. Gently introducing and educating employees in an extremely participative manner on appropriate workplace mobile phone usage.
3. Finding collaborative and collective solutions for addressing the issue across the organization. This was key since this process would build a high level of ownership and would ensure higher adherence to the formalized mobile ethics that would be subsequently formed.

RECOMMENDATIONS

The taskforce recommended the use of an organizational wide survey as the primary methodology to capture real time data. They felt that a survey questionnaire would address all the three requirements in a participative, anonymous and non – threatening manner.

The following areas and dimensions were suggested:

1. Frequency and extent of inappropriate mobile use
   To capture real time data on the frequency with which the employees have observed the listed improper mobile phone use at the workplace. The study would be across three dimensions:
   - Talking loudly and mobile phone ringing at inappropriate occasions
   - Discourtesy
   - Accessing, viewing and using inappropriate content

2. Perceived consequences of inappropriate mobile use
   Views of the employees on the perceived consequences of inappropriate mobile use at the workplace would be studied across various dimensions:
   - Effect on productivity
   - Compromising the Information Security of organizational data
   - Organizational reputation
   - Organization culture and ambience
   - Dangers of employee termination

3. Suggestions from employees towards tackling inappropriate mobile use at the workplace
   The views of the employees on the suggested ways to deal with improper mobile use at the workplace would be studied across the dimensions of:

- Doing nothing
- Self-discipline
- Posting Notices / Installing monitoring devices
- Formulating rules and regulations
- Redressal mechanisms required

This was subsequently presented to the senior management of the SKS Group who approved the plan for its simplicity, comprehensiveness and ease of implementation. The taskforce then got into the nuances of designing, testing and administering the organization survey on mobile usage at the workplace.

CONCLUSION

This case study provides a simple, effective and implementable roadmap towards addressing the growing realities and concerns on mobile ethics at the workplace. Rather than following a top down directive approach, inappropriate mobile usage at the workplace needs to be tackled in a participatory and collaborative approach to get the employees to trust the process and extend their cooperation. This would ensure that employees do not feel threatened apropos their freedom, flexibility and privacy with using their mobile phones at the workplace. At the same time the employees have the feeling of personal and organizational power to maintain organizational norms, civility and decorum.

QUESTIONS FOR DISCUSSIONS

1. What according to you were the possible outcomes of this study conducted at SKS Group?
2. Do you think this approach can be universally applied across all organizations?
3. Design a detailed questionnaire based on the survey areas and dimensions mentioned by the taskforce at SKS group?
4. Based on the case study, formulate some key rules and policies on mobile ethics at the workplace.

COMMUNICATION CONFUSION: HILL OUT OF A MOLE

AUTHOR BIO

Dr. Ruchi Tewari

Dr. Tewari is engaged as a Faculty, General Management, with over 18 years of academic and industry experience. She has worked in the area of General Management, exploring the Communication of Corporate Social Responsibility (CSR) for her Doctorate in Philosophy (Ph.D.); which she completed after an M.Phil. in English. She has done extensive research work in the area of CSR and has worked on various aspects of applied communication. Her professional horizon encompasses teaching communication and development related courses and guiding post-graduate students, presenting and publishing research papers in national and international conferences and journals, conducting trainings, completing projects and consultancy assignment for organizations.

She is an established trainer associated with several organizations in Ahmedabad where she conducts regular sessions as a part of the employee development programmes organized by them. She has conducted over 500 hours of training in various organizations like telecommunication (product and services), manufacturing, real estate and education.

Dr. Tewari has 20 publications in national and international academic journals and several chapters in edited books. She has also presented 15 conference papers in national and international conferences. She is an editorial review member for two national and one international peer-reviewed journal. She is a member of Asian Media and Information Centre (AMIC), Association of Business Communicators in India (ABCI), Public Relations Society of India (PRSI), Indian Society of Training and Development (ISTD), and is a regional coordinator of Society for Management and Behavioural Sciences.

Her areas of interest include corporate communication and responsible business activity.

Dr. Ritu Sharma

Dr. Sharma is currently engaged as an Assistant Professor and Head of Department, Psychology with Pandit Deendayal Petroleum University (PDPU) Gandhinagar. Dr. Sharma is a gold medallist, and holds a Ph.D. in Psychology. She has over 12 years of work experience in teaching, training and research; and is involved and effective in the complete gamut of academic activities – teaching, research and institutional development. Dr. Sharma is engaged with international and national research projects and training assignments in the areas of human behaviour, personality development and psychometric profiling. She has conducted several workshops and training programmes for the academia, corporate and NGOs in various areas of human behaviour and interpersonal effectiveness.

She has lectured extensively on various topics related to Application of Psychology in Industry and Society in national institutes. Currently she is also a project head from India for a study on "Women's Economic Empowerment in Asia: Psychosocial and Anthropological factors". She has widely published papers in journals of national and international repute. She has presented papers in several international and national level conferences both in India and overseas; and has represented university research work in various institutes in Europe and Australia. She is an Associate Life Member of Indian Association of Clinical Psychology. She is Member of Confederation of Indian Industry (Western Region), Indian Women Network (IWN) and International Economics Development and Research Center (IEDRC). She has been nominated as an Executive Council Member of Indian Association of Cognitive Behaviour Therapy, and as Board of studies members for two other Universities in Gujarat.

Executive Summary

Magnificence Infrastructure (MIL) is a newly established real estate company. It was started as a diversification arm of Readwell Publishers – a reputed and well performing publishing house. Magnificence was trying innovative ways to entice the residents of a Tier-II city in India. One of their key objectives was to service the customers who had taken possession and began to occupy 'Bliss', a 14 storey top-end luxury apartment. Magnificence was the first real-estate company to set-up an estate and complaint management department, which had its team of seven members stationed at Bliss to respond to the housekeeping and maintenance related complaints of the residents.

Their marketing campaign was built around the tag-line, 'luxury with warmth; comfort with ease'. The sales pitch carried a commitment to handle and sort complaints within 24 hours. The estate and complaint management department was geared to work in tandem with the project team comprising of engineers, plumbers, and carpenters etc. to handle customer complaints.

Six months after 75% of the 224 apartments (four flats per floor in a 14 floor building, with four such towers) were occupied, the estate and complaint management department was flooded with emails, phone calls and face to face complaints from the residents of Bliss. The management realized that their reputation could be compromised and this may lead to an adverse impact on the sales of other upcoming projects. The complaints also had a spill over effect and led to internal conflicts which were arising due to blame game between sales, estate and complaint management and project department. The top management of Magnificence decided to hire a consultant to handle the situation and help them find an appropriate solution to the problem.

Setting The Stage

Retired Colonel Abhijeet Singh Marwah finished an interaction with a group of residents of Bliss. It was an extremely hostile discussion. He had put to use all the courtesies and social ways he had picked up in his training in the army, but it seemed his gentle and social ways were not enough to pacify the agitated residents of Bliss. They walked out of the meeting grumbling and screaming, accusing Magnificence Infrastructure Ltd. (MIL) of having cheated them with false promises. They specifically mentioned to the colonel that the core attraction for buying a flat in Bliss was the promise of a well-kept residential colony which would be serviced and maintained professionally, and this promise was not kept.

INDUSTRY BACKGROUND

MIL had entered the real-estate industry with a promise to raise the bar and to ensure that they are pioneers in benchmarking best practices in the sector. According to a KPMG report (2016) it is estimated that the real estate sector will increase five-fold to reach USD 676 billion by 2025. Real-estate sector in this Tier-II town in western India are dominated by the unorganized sector. Infrastructure development in residential sector means building well-designed housing colonies furnished with all amenities like swimming pools, walking tracks, children park etc. While this attracts the residents to buy houses, once full occupancy is achieved, gradually over a period of time maintenance is compromised and amenities fall apart. Residents are then forced to care and manage their individual homes (ICICI, 2013). Most of these colonies throw garbage on the common internal roads, street lights are dysfunctional and other common zones like the children park etc. become areas of garbage and dump accumulation. There is a clear gap in true luxury housing segment where demand still continues to be high, but buyer expectations are not being met (Firstpost, 2013). The sector has seen considerable growth because the per-capita income in urban India is expected to triple from USD 2,800 in 2012 to USD 8,300 in 2028, with an annual movement of about 10 million people towards cities in India (GoI, 2011). The movement happens since the prospects of employment and better lifestyle seems more promising in the cities which are expected to contribute 70-75% of the country's GDP by 2025. (Cebr, 2013).

CASE DISCUSSION

One of the residents of Magnificence mentioned, "Our family moved from an old ill-maintained building to Bliss because MIL had promised a swanky and elite life-style which meant well-designed and well-maintained houses and common amenities". Most residents were happy with the way Magnificence was designed – both the houses and the amenities. Maintenance seemed to be the cause of concern.

Mr. Suraj Raj, the Managing Director of MIL had anticipated that the illogical boom in the real estate was over and that the housing market had begun to consolidate. Realizing builders need to think out of the box, he endeavored to provide services which surpasses usual customer expectations. This would help them attract new customers as well as retain current ones. Unfortunately MIL only had the experience of launching high-grade products. They realized that providing services required a completely different set of expertise, and they had no experience to handle it.

The residents were accusing MIL to be a 'cheat organization', and that it had failed to live up to its promises. Their accusations were that there was lack of courtesy and promptness in acknowledging the complaints registered, duplication of queries regarding clarifications about the complaints made at the estate department, and delays in handling the problems. Due to these reasons, they had to give constant reminders and report the complaints repeatedly. They felt MIL was apathetic and therefore they threatened the Colonel that they shall contact the Managing Director and complain about the shabby treatment which they were getting from the estate management department. Problems included leaking taps, short circuits in rooms, DTH system working intermittently etc. In addition to this, the common areas were constantly dirty and lights non-functional in the children's garden. One of the angered residents mocked the Colonel and said, "Why don't you also move in this luxury high end living to experience the atrocious services".

As the residents left in rage the colonel's ears were ringing with threats and accusations. He could also not help but reminisce about the innumerable occasions when his family had felt neglected and discussed with him how he was over-involved in work. They complained that as a result of the frustration that he faced due to his work schedule, he often expressed unjustified anger. Colonel Marwah felt hapless because he realized that he had failed to deliver in both his personal and professional relationships. As soon as he reached his office he received a call from the Mr. Suraj Raj, Managing Director, MIL. The Colonel was called for an immediate meeting at the MD's office and it now became clear that the issue of the dissatisfaction of the residents of Bliss had become critical.

The meeting between the MD and Colonel had a simple conclusion – the MD was highly disappointed with the colonel. He openly stated, "We hired you because we thought your defence background would help us handle public grievances with courtesy, but you have failed us." The Colonel attempted to state his side of the story, "My phone rings 24 hours and my mail box is full with complaints apart from the oral and written complaints they (residents) leave at the estate office at Bliss."

The MD understood the Colonel's problem, but remained worried. He was desperate to find a way to resolve the problem since Bliss was a flagship pioneer project launched in the market with great confidence and hope. He did not want the project to fail since it would affect future projects as well. Realizing that there is a root cause to every problem, he endeavoured to identify the root cause of this problem, and come up with a solution.

Resolution

The MD was keen to find a solution to this problem and so the very next day he called for a meeting of all the department heads. The clear objective was to brainstorm and find a way to fix the problem. The MD and Colonel were joined by both Head of Project, Mr. Paresh Vakil and Mr. Sudarhsan Iyer; and the Head of Marketing. While entering the boardroom, the Colonel heard the two Head of departments discussing how the estate management department was causing problems for everyone. The Colonel was distressed to hear this.

Once they all gathered, everyone put forth their points. Mr. Vakil stated that the team (site engineers, full time carpenters, plumbers, electricians and mason and daily wage workers engaged in adjoining construction sites) were called in for service at odd hours by the members of the estate department. A pertinent point put forward by Mr. Vakil was that the duplication in calls lead to redundancy in the process. Mr. Iyer reported that aggrieved customers had been calling the marketing team complaining that while the organization tried to appear as a customer-friendly organization, it was in fact insensitive to its customers.

After listening to different thoughts and opinions of the various heads, the MD realized that every department had a myopic point of view. They were concerned and worried only about the way in which the working of the estate department adversely impacted their own departments. Since none of them recommended any concrete solutions or plan of action, the MD suggested hiring an external consultant who would submit to them an objective report identifying the problem and recommending solutions. His suggestion received a unanimous acceptance. Within a fortnight, SRR consultants was hired.

SRR Conclusion: Hill Out of a Mole

The consultant team conducted a round of meetings with the entire team to validate the inputs provided by the MD in his briefing. They met the three-member estate team at Bliss and were surprised that each one of them said that they were over-worked, that there was no care for dignity and self-esteem in the organization, and that they were exploring opportunities outside MIL. They complained that they received calls from customers and the Colonel at odd hours of the day. They were always under pressure and over-worked. There were also frequent occasions when the estate team would realize that there was redundancy due to multiple communications received.

The consultant team analysed the situation and made the assessment on the following parameters:

- Nature of complaints segregated into usual and extra-ordinary.
- Time of complaint flow.
- Complaint Handling - method of registering the complaint, time taken to respond, coordination with various departments and closing of the complaint, distribution of complaints amongst executives at estate department.
- Role and responsibilities within the estate department about complaint handling.

They analysed the complaint record for the previous four weeks (Exhibit 1).

Exhibit 1: Initial Four Week Analysis of Written Complaints at Bliss

Day	Number of Complaints	Mode of registering the complaint	Time of registering the complain	Nature of the complaint (Usual / Extraordinary)	
Mon	6	Written	12:30 – 3:30 pm	Usual – 6	Ex – 0
Tue	4	Written	12:30 – 3:30 pm	Usual – 3	Ex – 1
Wed	8	Written	12:30 – 3:30 pm	Usual – 8	Ex – 0
Thu	5	Written	12:30 – 3:30 pm & 6:30 – 9:30 pm	Usual – 5	Ex – 0
Fri	5	Written	12:30 – 3:30 pm	Usual – 3	Ex – 2
Sat	9	Written	2:00 – 10:30 pm	Usual – 9	Ex – 0
Sun	15	Written	8:30 – 12:30 pm & 6:30 – 9:30 pm	Usual – 13	Ex – 2

Source: Authors

SRR was surprised when they matched these records with the number of complaints which each executive at the estate office was handling. Three executives were handling on average 34 complaints every week. Such a disproportionate match between the numbers were confounding. They were sure that there was some duplication somewhere. When SRR met the estate team with the complaint analysis of the last four weeks, one of the executives naively mentioned, "These are only written complaints which you have noted. What about the oral complaints and the ones which come directly from Colonel Sir and the project department?"

SRR consultants visited Bliss randomly over the entire week to track and classify the complaint according to the registration system.

- Modes of complaint registration (Oral, Written and through Off-sites channels).
- Relationship status of the owner to the person registering the complaint.
- Time of registration of complaint.
- New or repeat complaint. In case of a repeat complaint, details of the person registering the original complaint – time, mode and person in-charge with whom the complaint was registered.

SRR got back to Mr. Raj with their final report and key analysis (Exhibit 2).

Exhibit 2: Detailed Analysis of All Complaints Registered At Bliss

Day	Number of Complaints	Mode of registering the complaint (Written / Oral / Offsite)	New / Repeat	Time of Complaints
Mon	10	W – 6; O – 3; OS – 1	N – 5; R – 5	6:00 – 10:00 am; 12:30 – 3:30 pm & 6:00 – 7:30 pm
Tue	17	W – 4; O – 10; OS – 3	N – 7; R – 10	6:00 – 10:00 am; 12:30 – 3:30 pm & 6:00 – 7:30 pm
Wed	10	W – 8; O – 0 ; OS – 2	N – 6; R – 4	6:00 – 10:00 am; 12:30 – 3:30 pm & 6:00 – 7:30 pm
Thu	23	W – 5; O – 15 ; OS – 3	N – 12; R – 11	6:00 – 10:00 am 12:30 – 3:30 pm & 6:00 – 9:30 pm
Fri	8	W – 5; O – 3 ; OS – 0	N – 5; R – 3	6:00 – 10:00 am; 12:30 – 3:30 pm & 6:00 – 7:30 pm
Sat	11	W – 9; O – 1 ; OS – 1	N – 6; R – 5	2:00 – 10:30 pm
Sun	23	W – 15; O – 8 ; OS – 0	N – 14; R – 9	8:30 – 12:30 pm & 6:30 – 9:30 pm

Source: Authors

The problem was clear. In the absence of a formalized complaint registration system, all possible and available channels of communication were used by the residents at Bliss. Complaints were being registered by the same household and sometimes by the same person multiple times. They used multiple channels of communication and the estate team counted every complaint as a fresh complaint. This led to their inability to sort through complaints quickly, and work piled up. This in turn led to an over-worked team, a frustrated team leader, and annoyed and bitter colleagues.

When SRR probed the reasons from the various receivers who registered and entertained complaints, there was a uniform response, "To uphold our promise of luxury with warmth; comfort with ease." The estate team did not want to turn down a customer. This was an integral rule communicated to them multiple times by the company.

CONCLUSION

The complaint registration system needed to be formalized and turned into a complaint record system. SRR designed a template for a complaint record slip which necessarily had to be put in written at the estate office between 8:30 am – 2:00 pm. Post 2:00 pm, the complaints were registered with the next subsequent date. The estate team would spent the next two hours acknowledging complaints and coordinating with the project team for necessary support of service staff like carpenters, plumbers or electricians. Contact details of these service staff were shared with the residents by 9:00 pm and usual complaints were handled and resolved next morning between 8:00 am – 2:00 pm.

SRR managed to successfully isolate the problem and accordingly figure out a solution. The MD was extremely happy since there was no extra resource allocation required.

REFERENCES

Cebr (2013). Cebr's World Economic League Table. Retrieved October 13, 2016, from https://www.cebr.com/reports/world-economic-league-table-2015/

Crisil. (2016). Indian Real Estate Overview. Retrieved October 15, 2016, from www.crisil.com/pdf/capitalmarket/Industry-content.pd. Retrieved on 1st August, 2016.

Firstpost. (2013). Demand for luxury homes still intact despite plunging sales. Retrieved October 13, 2016, from http://www.firstpost.com/real-estate/ demand-for-luxury-homes-still-intact-despite- plunging-sales-527731.html

GoI. (2011). Census 2011. Retrieved August 5, 2016, from http://www.censusindia.gov.in/2011-common/census_2011.html

ICICI. (2013). Ahmedabad Residential Real Estate Overview. Retrieved October 5, 2016, from http://www.icicihfc.com/property_pdfs/ahmedabad-realestate-overview- march2012.pdf

KPMG. (2016). Real Estate (Regulation and Development) Bill, New Delhi. Retrieved October 20, 2016, from https://www.kpmg.com/IN/en/IssuesAndInsights/ArticlesPublications/Documents/Real-Estate-(Regulation-and-development) Bill, March 2016.pdf

Gautam: A Cultural Evangelist? A Cross-Cultural Context

Author Bio

Ruchi Pathak

Ruchi has done her MBA from MDU, Rohtak and is currently a full-time Ph.D. scholar at Amity International Business School, Amity University, Noida. Her broad area of research is HRM and Open Innovation. Ruchi carries a total of 5+ years of experience which includes including 2.5 years of experience as a Human Resource Consultant with Manpower Consultant, Delhi and 3 years of experience as Assistant Professor at Manav Rachna International University, Faridabad. She has to her credit 10 publications including research papers, book reviews and case studies. Her research interests are Innovation and HRM, Organizational Strategy, Business Models and Open Innovation.

Dr. R. Sujatha

Dr. Sujatha is an Associate Professor in the Department of Human Resource at Amity Business School with 12 years of teaching experience. She completed her Ph.D. in the year 2007 as a full time research scholar from the Department of Commerce, University of Madras with focus in the areas of Organizational Behavior and Human Resource Management. She has been a Research Associate with the Foundation for Sustainable Development, IIT Madras where she conducted research on *Costing of Health Care Interventions in the state of Tamil Nadu*, a project funded by W.H.O. Her current areas of research interest include Leadership, Intrapreneurship and Strategic Human Resource Management. She has to her credit 22 national and international conference papers, and 27 published research papers and cases. She has been the coordinator for the Stream Entrepreneurship at Amity University and was involved in the Uniform Course Coding System. She has been program coordinator for the MBA (Entrepreneurship) class of 2014 and 2015 and has mentored students of entrepreneurship. She has been actively engaged in academic process administration and university accreditation processes. She has delivered lectures to students of DBA program ISM Paris in topics of 'Doing Business in India'. She is a resource person in training programmes, orientation programmes and workshops organized by various bodies.

Dr. Puja Sareen

Dr. Puja Sareen is a Ph.D. in the area of Human Resource Management with a total of 15 years of in industry and academic experience. She was a University Topper in B.Com (H) and MBA. She has been certified by IICA, Ministry of Corporate Affairs as a Master Trainer for their Certificate Program in CSR. She has been associated with Amity Business School, Amity University, Noida as a faculty since 2014. She has conducted various soft skills training programs for students and corporate. She has published several papers in international and national journals and conference proceedings. Her research areas are Training and Development, e-HRM and HRIS. She has reviewed manuscripts for journals like IJHRM and IBME.

EXECUTIVE SUMMARY

Most of the organizations today recognize the need to manage cultural differences. International corporations have shown their inclination to capture markets, and are putting in constant effort to gain momentum and competitive advantage for business. This has increased the need to improve the level of knowledge and competencies of cross cultures to gain competitive advantage. The success of any international corporation is dependent on the managers playing "Global Leadership" roles. Leadership in global organizations is becoming complex and riskier and increased involvement of people from a diverse workforce. The challenge of a 'Global Leader' refers to the need to build awareness about cross-culturalism, country specific work ethic, managing the heterogeneity in demographics, understanding communications patterns, dealing with racial conflicts and individual differences and so on. Despite prominence of studies in the area of culture, organizational culture, cross culture, leadership and culture, change and culture; there is a dearth of literature in understanding the specific ways in which the "message of culture" in a structured and unstructured way is taken forward among the stakeholders by the actors, leaders and managers of the international organizations. The present case is built with this context to examine the role of a manager as a 'cultural evangelist' in an organization. This case explores how an Indian manager from Haitian, Global Corporation, China discovered those determinants of culture that can influence the competitiveness of the company and crucial elements of being a cultural evangelist. The secondary data was compiled through regular interaction with the Indian manager over a period of eight months.

SETTING THE STAGE

> **Employee:** I don't understand the purpose of the product A221.
> **Manager:** Oh! That's a burger brand. Americans eat a lot of beef and some like to burn their initials into their food with a red hot iron, before they eat.
> **Employee:** But why?

Manager: Well it's like a cattle brand, the thing you see to burn a symbol into a cow. Branding is how you keep track of your cow (*confused, why people are looking like this*).

Employee: (*Sad and amazed*) With a red-hot iron?

Manager: Yes

2nd Employee: But wouldn't the cow run away?

Manager: No, we do it on baby cows when they are small enough to hold them down (*everyone with a disgust on face and amazed*).

3rd Employee: Sir, I have a suggestion. You need to learn about India.

From the movie *Outsourced*

We understand from this conversation that one can realise the important role culture plays for businesses operating in international boundaries. Most of the organizations today recognise the need of managing cultural differences. International corporations have shown their inclination to capture markets, and are putting in constant effort to gain momentum and competitive advantage for business. This need has increased the need to improve the level of knowledge and competencies of cross cultures to gain competitive advantage. So, *'culture is an energy field – it affects everything in an organization for better or worse'*[1].

The success of any international corporation is dependent on the managers playing "Global Leadership" roles. Leadership in global organizations is becoming complex and riskier and increased involvement of people from a diverse workforce. The challenge of a 'Global Leader' refers to the need to build awareness about cross-culturalism, country specific work ethic, managing the heterogeneity in demographics, understanding communications patterns, dealing with racial conflicts and individual differences and so on. To prepare for global leadership roles it is very important for mangers to understand the concept of organizational culture: Macro and Micro determinants of culture. Organizational culture is "the set of shared, taken-for-granted implicit assumptions that a group holds and that determines how it perceives, thinks about, and reacts to its various environments" (Schein, 2011). It is a pattern of shared basic assumptions learned by a group as it solves its problems of external adaptation and internal integration (Schein, 2011). The concept of culture as borrowed from the discipline of anthropology

---

1   innovativecultures.org

has been variedly used in organizational studies. However, its function is broadly interpreted as a tool of organizational identity, social system and stability and / or a sense making tool for organizational members to generate organizational commitment and shaping up of their behavior. Many studies on organizations have clearly indicated that there is a noticeable influence of powerful culture on driving employee behavior to organizational goals and performance. Research in the past also concludes that strategy execution and implementation is an outcome of building a strong culture by leaders and managers (Schein, 2004). Therefore, it is realized that each leader ensures to shape the culture of the organizations through various mechanisms for bringing out those employee behaviors that are aligned to the organization's mission and philosophy.

Despite the prominence of studies in the area of culture, organizational culture, cross culture, leadership and culture, change and culture there is a dearth of literature in understanding the specific ways in which *"message of culture"* in a structured and unstructured way is taken forward among the stakeholders by the actors, leaders and managers of the international organizations. In fact, Schein (2011) highlights that the role and challenges of leadership within organizations are dependent on the way the individual manager and leader had conceived the culture. One cannot deny that a leader, whether formal or informal, can influence the behavior of employees in the way they articulate the organizational vision or mission, making meaning about external events such as competition, deliverables or issues of internal integration. The present case is built with this context to examine the role of manager as a *'cultural evangelist'* in organizations. An evangelist is a person who is a converter, propagandist or gospeller or a zealous advocate of a particular cause[2]. Researchers claim that the English word "evangelism" comes from the Greek word *euaggelion*. Most literally translated in the noun form, *euaggelion* means "gospel" or "good news."[3] This case explores how an Indian manager from Haitian, Global Corporation – China discovered those determinants of culture that can influence the competitiveness of the company and crucial elements of being a cultural evangelist. The secondary data was compiled through regular interaction with the Indian manager over a period of eight months. It is part of a project undertaken by the researchers in the area of open innovation.

---

2 https://www.google.co.in/#q=evangelist+etymology
3 https://carm.org/what-is-evangelism

CASE DISCUSSION

Human values are same universally, it is merely how we express them that makes us different when we compare values across countries. It never means we respect somebody more or we value something less. India and China, commonly referred to as "giants on the rise" or "important engines of the globalized economy", have become progressively competitive. Both have crossed one billion mark in terms of population and are developing rapidly. However, there are apparent differences, and their unique characteristics bring competitiveness in the way organizations function in these countries. India differs from China on various fundamental dimensions, demography and democracy being key. China has been built on infrastructure, investment and manufacturing, while India has barely scratched the surface on these.

1. Chinese corporate culture:

In China the culture emphasizes on meticulous work. Socializing after work is very much part and parcel of the culture. Business relationships are solidified after personal interactions. Rank is extremely important in business relationships. One must therefore keep rank differences in mind when communicating with colleagues irrespective of the setting. The Chinese prefer face-to-face meetings rather than written or telephone communication. Gender bias is non-existent in business. There is a distinct line between professional and personal lives in China, so one should not discuss business at meals or any other type of social event.

2. Indian corporate culture:

India is a very different country than China on many fundamental dimensions, demography and democracy being key. India has its own unique and subtle manner in which business is conducted. Success can depend on an appreciation and understanding of the cultural aspects in addition to patience and a high level of long-term commitment and personal attention and involvement. Establishing and maintaining strong relationships with Indian business associates is fundamental to successful business in India[4].

---

4   http://www.sourcingfocus.com/site/opinionscomments/
understanding_indian_culture_for_successful_business/

3. Comparison with Geert Hofstede's cultural dimensions:

In terms of cultural differences, when compared on a Hofstede model, there are both similarities and differences that are visible. Exhibit 1 shows India vs. China based on Geert Hofstede model[5]. Power distance, an important dimension in the Hofstede's model, describes the extent to which less powerful members expect and accept unequal power distribution within a culture. Both India and China score high on this dimension, demonstrating a respect for hierarchy and a top-down structure in organizations. The subordinate-superior relationship tends to be polarized. In terms of Individualism / Collectivism, China is a highly collectivist culture where people act in the interests of the group and not necessarily of themselves. In-group considerations are very important in organizations. India is a society with both collectivistic and individualist traits.

Figure 1: Geert Hofstede Model comparison – India vs. China

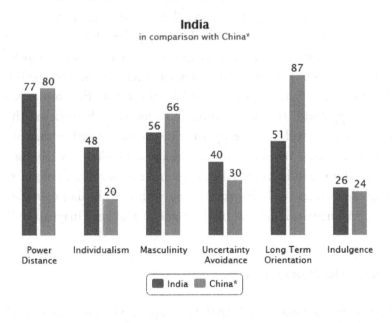

Source: Hofstede

---

5   https://geert-hofstede.com/india.html

Both countries are close in terms of being a masculine society and in terms of visual display of success and power. On the dimension of uncertainty avoidance, China scores lower than India. The adherence to laws and rules may be flexible to suit the actual situation and pragmatism is a fact of life. In terms of long term orientation, China scores higher than India in this dimension, reflecting a very pragmatic culture. There is a strong propensity to save and invest, thriftiness, and persistence in achieving results.

Haitian in India

After operating their business through their partner Electronica for a few years in India, Haitian took a decision to enter the Indian market directly. In 2011 Haitian opened their subsidiary Zhafir Plastics Machinery India Pvt. Ltd. in India with a central office setup in Mumbai. They registered their local office in the year 2012.

Gautam was an exceptional performer at Electronica and had set benchmarks through his performance. When Limin came to India in the capacity of General Manager, India, Limin poached him from Electronica and appointed him as an Area Manager with an increased compensation. Having an excellent personal and professional relation by then with Limin, Gautam immediately joined Zhafir after resigning from Electronica. Gautam was very happy with this new profile and venture as he believed that it is always preferable working directly with the company rather than working with intermediaries. By now Haitian had already ended their contract with Electronica for the Indian dealership. After more than a decade of successfully running the business in India, they set up with their Indian manufacturing facility in Ahmedabad, Gujarat by the name of Haitian Huayuan India Pvt. Ltd.

Gautam – The Protagonist

Having worked with AAR AAR Technoplast, Gautam's technical know-how of injection moulding machines was excellent. On completion of his first year at AAR AAR he was managing over 50 production labour on shop floors. After spending little over a year at shop floor, in mid-2004 he joined Electronica Machines Tools Ltd., now Electronica Plastic Moulding Division, as a sales executive. The company had been a local supplier of Haitian (China's top injection moulding machine manufacturer) in India. Haitian's service engineer Limin kept visiting India on several occasions to handle critical machine issues in India at customer locations. Gautam regularly accompanied Limin. Since both of them were hard-working, and eager to learn from each other, they shared an excellent rapport. Gautam learnt most of the organizational stories, myths and beliefs about Haitian from Limin. He would then pass these cultural learnings to his colleagues at Haitian India.

Gautam indicated the challenges of how the concept of culture for organizations that function between boundaries vary. Every organization develops distinctive beliefs and values. These cultural manifestations get reflected in various forms. Exhibit 1 captures the various determinants of organizational culture in Haitian, as a global organization. The framework investigates the differences and similarities among these variables in Haitian China and Haitian India. The country's culture in terms of business is also compared.

Exhibit 1: Geert Hofstede Model Comparison – India vs. China

S. No.	Determinants of Culture	China based organization	Haitian in China	Indian Organization	Haitian in India
1	**Core value**	Low cost	Quality	Good profit	Quality
2	**Purposefulness**				
	Customer Focus	Yes	Yes	Yes	Yes
	Market Focus	No	Yes	Somewhat	Yes
	Profit Focus	Somewhat	Somewhat	Yes	Somewhat
3	**Leadership**	N o	Yes	Yes	Yes
4	**Conflict handling mechanism**	No	Yes	Yes	Yes
5	**Negotiations**	Yes	Yes	Yes	Yes
6	**Ethics**	No	Yes	Yes	Yes
7	**Employee Participation**	No	Yes	No	Yes
8	**Customer Focused Strategies**	Yes	Yes	Yes	Yes

9	Management Support				
	Networking 360	No	Yes	Yes	Yes
	Access to resources	Yes	Yes	Yes	Yes
	Information sharing	No	Yes	Yes	Yes
	Control Mechanism	No	Yes	No	Yes
	Evidence of Bureaucracy	Yes	No	Yes	No
10	Space for innovation				
	Freedom to experiment	Yes	No	No	No
	Risk Behaviour	No	Yes	No	Yes
	Trust	Yes	Yes	Yes	Yes
11	Role behaviours encouraged				
	Open communication	No	Yes	Yes	Yes
	Decision Making	Yes	Yes	Yes	Yes
	Autonomy	No	Yes	Yes	Yes
12	Organizational Change	Yes	Yes	Yes	Yes

Source: Authors

As a cultural evangelist the Indian managers helped the researchers to analyse the determinants. A 'Yes' indicates similarity in the practices followed and a 'No' indicates the challenges for the Indian counterpart in playing the role of a cultural evangelist.

LEARNINGS

The first thing Gautam did at Haitian India was to ensure that the workforce grows and is retained. Gautam felt that cultural diversity refers to dealing with the perceptions and views of one another, and he believed it is a predisposition of thoughts. He felt that culture can lead or limit interaction between two individuals. Managing in diverse environment can be easily smoothened through extensive communication, adapting to what other culture has and dealing with the required changes. There are also some inherent challenges. For instance communication can be hindered by linguistic variations, adaptability can be hindered by limited knowledge about other culture, and not adapting to changes as well as perceptions and culture differences.

Broadly, what helped him the most was the organization's attitude for openness. He also made an effort to learn more about other Haitian's corporate culture and people as he felt cultural competence was required to deal in a cross cultural environment. He endeavoured to help them understand and ask for help on the matters which he was unable to understand. He also felt that social proximity / outdoor trips are a good idea to know and understand people from different cultures. Haitian has a policy of sending its best performers from India every year on an official trip to China followed by social gatherings within Haitian to meet and know people. Gautam narrates that "when we know that we have to deal with people from a different culture, a "new normal" attitude works – and one should not worry about asking questions." He well understood that his ultimate role is to rally people to achieve the organizational goal.

Gautam believes in paying attention to all those organizational aspects that are followed by Haitian China. He mentioned that Limin always ensures to adopt all the measurement and control mechanisms similarly as Haitian China. Gautam demonstrates in his role behaviour that customers are important for business. As per the symbolic frame and socialization process to maintain culture, Gautam rewards innovative behaviour of employees. He ensures to coach average performers. Gautam ensures to give realistic and actionable targets to his subordinates. He reviews performances regularly and provide critical feedback to them. The customers are also encouraged to speak up on business initiatives. This has led for productive working relationships in B2B marketing[6].

---

6   http://shawnhunter.com/jeffrey-pfeffer-on-creating-performance-culture/

CONCLUSION: FRAMEWORK FOR LEADERS TO BE A CULTURAL EVANGELIST

The role of leadership is to understand, create, and communicate in symbolic terms and help people to understand the organization and the meaning of their involvement with the organization. Gautam, the protagonist of this case, has executed 'Global Leadership' through translating the objectives of Haitian China in India through various mechanisms. The framework shown in Exhibit 2 highlights the same.

Exhibit 2: Framework for Leaders to Be a Cultural Evangelist

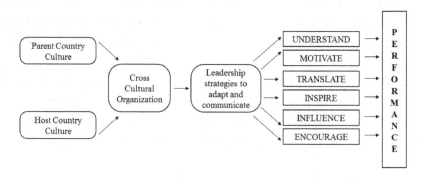

Source: Authors

A serious examination of the determinants of culture identifies the various aspects on which a global manager must concentrate in order to bridge the gap for global organizations, while operating in more than one boundary. It also implies that every good company and its managers need to know the full range of opportunities from organizational structure, technology, leadership, power, communication and so on in the process of conveying the same meaning about organizational culture. Taking it a step further, a cultural evangelist must not only gospel the message but translate, inspire and encourage people around them to follow the organizational culture.

REFERENCES

Schein, E.H (2004). *Organizational Culture and Leadership, Third edition*. San Francisco: Jossey-Bass.

Schein, E. H. (2011). *Leadership and Organizational Culture*. New York, NY: Wiley.

[The researchers intend to acknowledge Mr. Gautam Pant, Regional Manager-North for sharing cross cultural learnings and leadership experiences. We also thank Haitian Huayuan India for permitting us to interview Mr. Gautam Pant. The case is intended only for classroom discussions. The opinions and inputs do not intend to illustrate effective or ineffective handling of managerial situations.]

Employee Churn:
The Inevitable Challenge

Author Bio

Shreya Bhatia

Shreya Bhatia is presently pursuing MBA in Human Resources from Amity Business School, Noida. During her graduation, she has hosted various events like the 'Corporate Meet and CSR Awards 2013', AGBS youth fest Elation 2014 and has participated in Punjab University Fest. She has been an active volunteer at CII-Young India and is a member of Bharat Soka Gakkai. She completed her internship at Tata Teleservices and worked with the talent management team. Her areas of interest include understanding and formulating business strategy, organizational development and effectiveness, social emotional learning and psychometrics. She also has a keen interest in lifestyle writing and has won several calligraphy and debate competitions.

Hargovind Khattar

Mr. Hargovind Kakkar is an Assistant Professor in the areas of Compensation and Reward Management and Managing Business Process Outsourcing at Amity Business School. He has an MBA with specialization in Human Resource from Amity Business School. He is a Six Sigma Green Belt certified professional from BSI. He also holds a DNIIT – two year certification from NIIT. He is pursuing Ph.D. in Management from University Business School, Punjab University, Chandigarh. In his corporate experience, he has worked in various capacities as a manager, trainer and a consultant for ITES and consulting companies with outsourcing and off shoring business delivery models. While discharging these duties, he was involved in the strategy team. His training experience includes conducting training programs for corporate, retired officers of armed forces and volunteers of CWG 2010.

EXECUTIVE SUMMARY

The Indian telecommunications industry is among the most flourishing in Asia. India is at present the world's second largest telecommunications market after China. Development of business over the years has driven the legislature to concede more players on the field, prompting a genuine value war to seek greater control and a larger piece of the pie. This eventually prompted diminishing revenue per client, triggered agitation and led to increased employee churn. Managing employee churn has turned into a noteworthy challenge for the telecom business, particularly in India. This has driven organizations to concentrate on procedures to expand employee engagement and mitigate churn. The motivation behind this case is to understand the possible reasons giving rise to employee churn within one year and studying how Fesco Ltd. constructed a strategic retention framework in order to curb the issue and achieve industry benchmark.

SETTING THE STAGE

Fesco Ltd. embarked its journey in 1997 with its headquarters in Delhi. Over the years the company has faced a variety of challenges. Recent data has decisively demonstrated that employee churn in the company is a significant, far-reaching issue since a long time. When an employee leaves his job, it is considered as churn by some associations. Others see it is as being poached by a new organization – which can refer to a professional move by the employee for monetary development, career progression etc. Today when a valuable employee leaves, it causes a substantial aggravation in the company. It is critical to comprehend and deal with the churn, as hiring a top-notch employee and the costs involved in training are substantial.

Fesco aimed to achieve the following objectives:

1. To study the attrition rate of its employees in Punjab, Himachal Pradesh and Haryana.
2. To study the factors that compels an employee to leave the organization.
3. To propose a framework to overcome attrition.

ORGANIZATIONAL BACKGROUND

Fesco Ltd. is a thriving high tech telecom organization that has a workforce of more than 500 employees under the Punjab, Himachal Pradesh and Haryana circles. Operating in a highly competitive market, the staff is transient. The Human Resources function of the company is divided into separate departments - Talent Acquisition, Talent Management, Employee Engagement and Personnel Management. The talent management and employee engagement departments are interlinked.

An operational meeting held in 2015 highlighted the prime concern of diminishing sales staff within one year of employment along with significantly high level of attrition noticeable in marketing and customer service departments. The company's Vice President Human Resource Mr. Vinod Sharma solicited help from the Human Resource head Ms. Meena Goswami who was tasked with improving retention. Meena checked the exit interview data and conducted a study with the objective to achieve a superior level of understanding about employees who leave the organization within a year. She characterized the data into three parts:

1. Attrition by Departments
2. Attrition by Type of employees
3. Attrition by Work experience

CASE DISCUSSION

As indicated by the organization's information base, Meena discovered that attrition was a major concern in the following departments: Customer service, Sales and Marketing. Further analysis of the data was done, taking pre-paid and post-paid employees. Attrition percentages were then calculated.

The total number of employees who left the organization within one year was found out to be 95 out of 515; therefore the total attrition rate was 18%. The steady loss rate was outstandingly higher in the sales department viz. 42% - most prominent among the fresh hires. The next department with observable churn was the customer service department at 32%, including the new hires and laterals. It was noticeable that the employees having 1-2 years of work experience were leaving the organization prior to those who had more than two years of work experience.

Meena also recorded the reasons given by the employees who had decided to leave the organization. It was a very important part of the study as she conducted a Pareto analysis and found out that 20% causes were giving rise to 80% of the problems in the organization. These problems were:

- Current boss and their style of working
- Work-life imbalance

Exhibit 1 shows all the problems that surfaced from the analysis.

Exhibit 1: Reasons Given By Employees to Leave the Organization

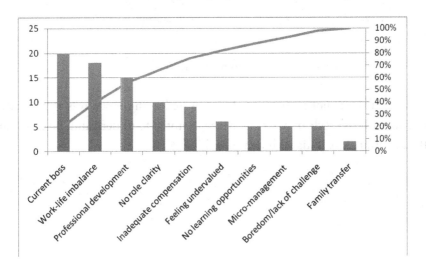

Source: Authors

She also decided to do a fishbone analysis in consensus with the managers in order to find out the root cause of the problems. The major problem areas identified are shown in Exhibit 2.

Exhibit 2: Major Problem Areas Leading To Employee Churn

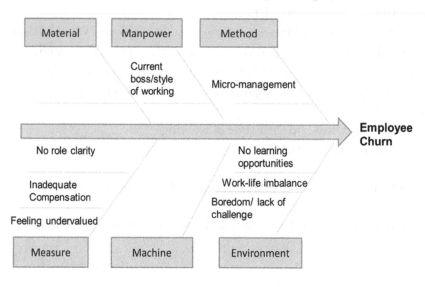

Source: Authors

One of the major reasons employees were leaving Fesco was attributed to the current boss's style of working. Meena wanted to understand the cause and effect relationship. This is shown in Exhibit 3.

Exhibit 3: Cause and Effect Relationship

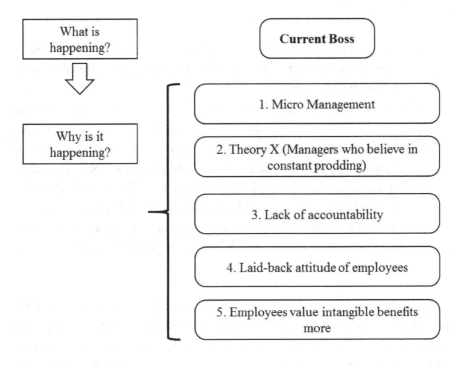

Source: Authors

After studying this in detail, she observed that the managers were following micro-management as a control method because the organization consisted of Theory X managers. These managers therefore believed in constant interference of the employees work. They did this because they felt that there was lack of accountability as the employees had a laid-back attitude, and because apparently a huge chunk of employees valued intangible benefits more. With the millennials joining in the company (45% of the total workforce) who are a lot more difficult to retain, it was perceptible that money was not the only motivating factor for them. They wanted to know about the internal opportunities available to them within the company.

Alternatives

In order to increase employee retention and satisfaction, she devised a strategic retention framework which was termed as 'Structure of Engagement

Anatomy' and included development of an effective organizational culture. This consists of:

1. Position Fit: This focuses on realistic job previews at the time of recruitment in order to ensure selective hiring, and extension of the on-boarding process.
2. Culture Fit: This originally consisted of weekly focus group discussions with the managers, stay interviews in order to facilitate one on one conversation to reduce the manager/employee gaps, monthly workshops on reducing power distance, renewed compensation packages and the bell curve method for performance appraisal. These methods had to be abandoned. Instead 360° feedback system has been adopted.
3. Career Fit: This is aimed at retaining the generation Y employees which is broken down into development planning, defining career path, and succession planning.

This framework was discussed with the top management and the managers in order to be implemented successfully to achieve improved retention. Measurement will be done on the basis of number of self-managed teams, quality circles available, organizational citizenship behaviour, and also how employees take initiative for new projects. She also understood that transparency in corporate communications could be an important tool in solving various internal problems. It is imperative to know what method a company deploys to communicate important organizational strategies and their impact on different departments, as well as employee perception and contribution i.e. internal psychological process. Each employee and manager will get a better understanding of being on the same page while striving for increased organizational productivity and effective accomplishment of goals.

QUESTIONS FOR DISCUSSION:

1. Do you think it is a cause of concern when employees in a company quit their jobs within one year of employment? State reasons for the same.

2. Are the existing strategies redundant in the dynamic telecom sector? If yes, what could be an innovative approach to reduce employee churn?
3. Going further, is there a possibility that talented employees are switching to different industries altogether and just not within the telecom sector? If yes, suggest measures to retain them.

Global Managers:
Facing The World

Author Bio

Dr. Reena Shah

Dr Reena Shah is a Ph.D. from Nirma University and a post graduate from Gujarat University. She holds over 17 years of experience with 14 years in academia and 3 years in the corporate. In her corporate stint, Dr. Shah was engaged in portfolio management for high net worth clients, which gave her an exposure to real time financial research and publication of market reports. With nearly a decade and half in academia she has managed and supervised the entire gamut of academic responsibilities including administrative responsibilities like program coordination of a nationally reputed management institute. Her area of teaching and research is Human Resource Management, Organisation Behaviour and Communication.

Dr. Shah has attended workshops and faculty development programs on Case Method in Management Teaching conducted by IIM, Ahmedabad and other esteemed academic institutions. She is a certified trainer by Thomas International and is frequently invited as a guest speaker and subject expert by members of the academic fraternity. Dr Shah has attended a number of national and international conferences and has publications in the research area of work-life balance. Her doctoral research has resulted in the construction of a unique scale measuring work-life balance and its antecedents in the Indian context. She was chosen by her institute to lead a project titled 'Single Window Industry Clearance in the State of Gujarat', jointly commissioned by Gujarat Chamber of Commerce and Industry and the Industry Ministry (Gujarat).

INTRODUCTION

Raj Bansal, a young Business Development Executive working with JPJ Pharma's London division, was walking on the streets of the sprawling metropolis. He contemplating the situation in front of him. He had received two calls earlier in the day that were forcing him to come to a life changing decision. One call was from his mother who had called from India, asking him to finalize the date of his wedding; and the other call was from one of the JPJ's biggest competitor ZKY, with a job offer to head the international business development operations in Germany. While walking down the familiar streets of London, Raj remembered how at one time this city was unknown and mysterious to him – about which he had only read in novels or seen in movies. Raj reminisced about the critical career choice that he had made in the past and the chain of events that led to his current dilemma.

SETTING THE STAGE

It had been four years and two months since Raj started working with JPJ, a leading pharmaceutical organization based out of Delhi. Raj had completed his graduation from Delhi College of Pharmacy in 2007 and was one of the first ones to get placed because of a sound academic background and good communication skills. Raj was 26 years old and hailed from the northern Indian city of Chandigarh. He had joined as a product management trainee and rose to be a product manager within a span four years. During his tenure, he had proved to be a star performer and was considered to be very hard-working by his superiors. Among his peers, he was found to be outgoing and reliable, someone who was ready to come forward and help others in need. His boss Mr. Firoz Wadia took special interest in Raj and was often heard remarking to others, "This boy is going to go a long way. It is not just his ability to do his work well but it's his attitude which makes him stand out." JPJ had a culture of recognizing and celebrating talent that was backed with performance and hence Raj, who had joined as product management trainee, rose to the position of product manager within a span of four years.

Organization Background

JPJ is in the pharmaceutical business since last 40 years and has the history of being consistently ranked among the top pharmaceutical companies of India. The company is known to be a trend setter in the Indian pharmaceutical industry. The organization's competitive edge comes from having sophisticated research and development competence, world class manufacturing facilities and widespread domestic as well as international market presence. Three of the company's state of art manufacturing facilities are located in popular pharmaceutical destinations of India – Gujarat, Himachal Pradesh and Sikkim. The domestic market was catered through SBU (Strategic Business Units) organized on therapeutic lines and a distribution network designed to have nationwide reach. The company is among the few acknowledged Indian pharmaceutical majors to recognize the importance of research and development in the post 2005 GATT (General Agreement of Trade and Tariff) era and invests heavily in the area of research and development.

Case Description

A new era was ushered in the Indian pharmaceutical industry when India became signatory to GATT recognizing product patents from January 2005. Since then India had emerged as a major supplier of pharmaceutical products worldwide. Pharmaceutical industry attained third position in the world in terms of production volume, and in terms of value it was ranked at fourteen.[7] The Indian pharmaceutical industry owes a lot of its growth to the Patent Act of 1970. Post-independence, the Indian pharmaceutical industry was predominantly led by the multi-nationals. With the agenda of boosting public healthcare, the Indian government began encouraging domestic pharmaceutical companies. The government enacted the Patent Act of 1970 that recognized only 'process patents'. This resulted into very rapid development of bulk drug industry as India possessed expertise in chemistry skills. Over the years, India became the leading producer of bulk drugs, now called Active Pharmaceutical Ingredients (APIs). In late seventies, India

---

7   Annual Report of Department of Pharmaceutical, Government of India.
     [http://pharmaceuticals.gov.in/sites/default/files/AnnualReport201415.pdf]

became net exporter of pharmaceutical products compared to its earlier status as net importer.

Under 'process patent' protection, the Indian pharmaceutical companies could lower the prices of their products through reverse engineering, while the multinational pharmaceutical companies which had to bear high research cost could not reduce their prices. Additional Government interventions in form of DPCO (Drug Price Control Orders) and higher import tariffs made the Indian market unattractive for the multinationals companies and therefore, they gradually went out of India and the domestic companies started replacing them in the pharmaceutical market. Exhibit 1 shows the shift in market share from multinational pharmaceutical companies to Indian pharmaceutical companies.

Exhibit 1: Pharmaceutical Industry: Market share
of Indian and Multinational companies

Year	Market Share of Domestic Companies	Market Share of Multinationals Companies
1947	NIL	100 %
1970	20 %	80 %
1991 onwards	67 %	33 %

Source: Annual Report 2008-09, Department of Pharmaceuticals, GOI

The economic reforms initiated in 1991 made India a party to GATT (General Agreement on Trade and Tariffs) and accordingly, by 1st January 2005, the industry had to shift to the 'product patent' regime being followed globally. After the compliance with 'product patent', the industry witnessed a new spell of growth and the Indian pharmaceutical companies turned into global players. The global presence came through two ways - first, through mergers and acquisitions of Indian and overseas companies to gain readymade access to patented products; and second, through consolidation and investment in research and development which enhanced their capabilities of developing new products.

In statistical terms, the Indian pharmaceutical industry holds a significant position in the global pharmaceutical market accounting for 10% of global exports in volume terms and 1.4% in value terms. The vast difference in the volume and value terms clearly illustrate the low cost competitive advantage of the Indian pharmaceutical industry that made it into one of the leading export sectors of India. The export and import figures are shown in Exhibit 2.

Exhibit 2: Exports and Imports of Pharmaceutical Industry

Year	Export of Pharmaceuticals Products (In USD billion)	Import of Pharmaceuticals Products (In USD billion)	Difference between Exports and Imports (In USD billion)
2011-12	838	22	816
2012-13	926	26	900
2013-14	1062	28	1034

Source: Annual Report 2014-15, Department of Pharmaceuticals, GOI

Manufacturing cost in India is about 40% lower than United States. Easy availability of raw material base and skilled manpower have been instrumental in making India one of the lowest manufacturing costs destination. Indian pharmaceutical products are exported to over two hundred companies. Out of these, the largest exporter of Indian pharmaceutical products is the US. Exports to UK also have shown a double digit growth rate.[8]

International Venture

It was in this changing scenario that JPJ also forayed into international markets. The company decided to take the route of having fully owned subsidiaries in upcoming pharmaceutical markets as well as into well-established markets that were partially regulated. The company first entered the US market followed by Germany and Russia. Looking at the rising potential it ventured into the UK in 2010 by establishing a fully owned subsidiary, having its registered office in London. Mr. Kishore Verma, who had been with

8   Pharmaceutical Export Promotion Council of India - Media reports. [http://pharmexcil.com]

the company for a long time and had extensive experience of international marketing, was put in charge of the London office. All other employees were hired locally. The company believed that talented people who had proved their loyalty to the company would be in a better position to lead the company in the overseas market. Sending people who had complete knowledge about the organisation, its products and the culture would ensure that uniform values and culture was established in all their offices across the globe. The company's experience of reliable communication between the head office and international offices in US, Germany and Russia had reinforced this belief.

In a short span of time, the London office was able to establish an excellent reputation in the UK and neighbouring markets and in this subsidiary showed a strong growth trajectory, as shown in Exhibit 3. The company at this stage needed more people to sustain the pace of growth. The functions carried out by Mr. Verma were getting too large for him to handle single handed. He required someone who could exclusively focus on business development. A request was sent to the corporate office to send additional staff.

Exhibit 3: Percentage of Domestic and International Sales of JPJ

Source: Authors

International Career Opportunity

In the Indian office, after working with JPJ for about four years, Raj felt his career stagnating as there were some opportunities that did not come his way because of not having a management degree. He decided to pursue an MBA and got admission in India's premier business school in South India. When he put in his papers, his manager Mr. Wadia dissuaded him from leaving the organisation to pursue an MBA. He offered him the Business Development position in the London office. The new position entailed higher responsibility and better pay package in comparison to the product manager position in India.

Mr. Wadia explained, "The prime responsibility of this position is to identify and develop opportunities in UK. This not only means a big leap in your career but it also means you get into mainstream management without the need to do your MBA." Raj was not prepared for this, and immediately reacted, "Thank you very much Sir! But I have never handled such a task, and will might find the challenge of handling an international market daunting." Mr. Wadia replied, "Don't worry about that. I am aware your capabilities and hence I am positive you will do well. Besides, I am acquainted with Mr. Kishore Verma at the London office. He is a very nice person and he will help you to get established. Let me do one thing, let me mail you the details of this position and you think about it, seek your family's opinion and let me know."

Raj had never been out of India, and was excited with the offer, which not only offered a great job profile and salary, but also gave him the opportunity to live and work overseas. Moreover he parents were still working, and were not dependent on him. Raj took his parent's advice and accepted the offer, in the process deferring his plans of pursuing his MBA. When the news of Raj's overseas assignment spread in the office, Dhiren Mallik, who had also joined JPJ approximately at the same time as him, came down to visit Raj. Dhiren, "Congratulations! I heard the news that you are offered a great position in our London office." Raj responded in an elated state, "Thanks! It was an opportunity that I never expected." Dhiren was curious to know the duration of this assignment and when Raj was likely to be back. To this Raj expressed his uncertainty, "As such there is nothing which is specifically mentioned, everything is very vague since the business there is relatively new and the scope of this assignment is also difficult to ascertain at this stage. However, looking at the cost involved, I guess I will be there for at least a couple of years."

Dhiren continued, "I guess only a few people were aware of this opening. It seems like a good opportunity. What were the criteria for selection? Did they take a special interview or something?" Raj described about how his resignation had resulted in this offer being made to him. Dhiren expressed his surprise that no special test was taken before the offer was made. He however anticipated that a rigorous training would definitely be given to Raj before he left. Raj expressed his doubts about the same since he was required to join the London office within a fortnight. He added, "Hey, I am only going to London! How difficult can it be? I am sure language and other such communication issues are not likely to come up hence a formal training as such may not be needed."

As predicted, the fortnight was really hectic for Raj as he had to assign all his pending assignment to others, apply for work visa and other formalities, and visit home to meet his parents.

The London Experience

Upon reaching London, Raj was thrilled. His team threw him a welcome party in which he managed get along well with everyone. Mr. Verma was also very warm and welcoming, and in spite of his very hectic schedule asked Raj to come to him whenever he needed anything. The London office was situated in the center of the bustling city of London and the excellent public transport facilities made everyday commute to work convenient. At work too, most of the people he worked with were very courteous and were ready to help him learn the ropes. He explored the place like a tourist, and some of the historical places and monuments made him revisit the history topics that he had studied when he was in school. He absolutely fell in love with the people, food, and; culture but most importantly his 'work'.

Four weeks later, his excitement started dwindling. Though he had been away from his home in Chandigarh for the past eight and a half years, it was for the first time that he was missing his family and friends back home. The snow seemed never ending and the weather was always gloomy. The need to stay constantly indoors both at the office and his room was very depressing. Packaged Indian food was very expensive, and going out to eat at an Indian restaurant was so exorbitant that it was unthinkable. Major portion of his salary – about 40% or so – went into taxes and one-third of the balance went as rent.

He felt at a disadvantage due to his accent, and often was unable to comprehend the meaning of what was being said, largely because of his unfamiliarity with the British accent and also because of the lack of understanding about the underlying communication patterns. Now that his welcome was over, he found people to be cold and very formal. His colleagues restricted their interaction to office work. None of his colleagues had invited him to their house; in fact he hardly knew anything about their family. He missed the warmth and companionship of his colleagues in India. He became quiet and did his unenthusiastically. Time zone difference made him all the more depressed. His parents back home were under the impression that he was busy and hence even they did not call up frequently.

He was assigned a work-buddy, but he was not comfortable sharing his thoughts. Mr. Wadia, his manager in India, picked up some of the hints and took charge of the situation. He reached out to him and made him visit the organizational therapist in London. Raj was reluctant. He thought that he would either be ridiculed by the team back in India. With a lot of hesitation, Raj gathered up courage and went ahead with the therapy, and while he was not articulate in the beginning, he soon started sharing his feelings. The therapy sessions reminded Raj of the objective with which he had come to London, and he gradually got past his home-sickness.

Soon after, Raj established a routine for himself. He picked up cooking as a hobby. He started following the local news and taking interest in the domestic affairs of UK. This gave him enough material to socialize.

Conclusion: Moving Ahead

Four years down the line, Raj has settled very well in London and has made a trustworthy name for himself in the UK pharmaceutical market. He has virtually turned second-in-command at the London office. Mr. Verma was likely to shift back to India in a year or two, and in all probability Raj would take over as his replacement.

Raj also got engaged to Radhika during one of his trips to India. Nearly a year has passed since the engagement, and both the families were now getting eager to set the date for the wedding.

Raj is at crossroads. If he continues with his job with JPJ in the London office, it would mean waiting for at least two years for Mr. Verma to move back to India. Moreover, this would mean that Radhika would have to sacrifice her career in India and start afresh in London. If he asks for an assignment to move back to the Indian office at JPJ, there is lack of surety about his position in the Delhi office. Most of the people who were working with him earlier had moved up the corporate ladder, and also Raj was unsure if there was any vacancy in the corporate office that matched his competencies. Raj weighted these options and contemplated if he had any other choices besides these.

WINDS OF CHANGE: UPROOTING THE FOUNDATION

AUTHOR BIO

Dr. Ekta Sharma

Dr. Sharma is engaged as a full-time faculty with Ahmedabad University's Amrut Mody School of Management. She has been engaged in academics for over a decade. Dr. Sharma completed her doctoral degree from Rajasthan University, Jaipur, after she cleared UGC-NET.

She has to her credit several academic publications in national and international journals of repute and has presented papers in national and international conferences. She has served as a member of the reviewer committee for established organizations like Academy of Management and is on the board of four national and one international journal.

Dr. Ruchi Tewari

Dr. Tewari is engaged as a Faculty, General Management, with over 18 years of academic and industry experience. She has worked in the area of General Management, exploring the Communication of Corporate Social Responsibility (CSR) for her Doctorate in Philosophy (Ph.D.); which she completed after an M.Phil. in English. She has done extensive research work in the area of CSR and has worked on various aspects of applied communication. Her professional horizon encompasses teaching communication and development related courses and guiding post-graduate students, presenting and publishing research papers in national and international conferences and journals, conducting trainings, completing projects and consultancy assignment for organizations.

She is an established trainer associated with several organizations in Ahmedabad where she conducts regular sessions as a part of the employee development programmes organized by them. She has conducted over 500 hours of training in various organizations like telecommunication (product and services), manufacturing, real estate and education.

Dr. Tewari has 20 publications in national and international academic journals and several chapters in edited books. She has also presented 15 conference papers in national and international conferences. She is an editorial review member for two national and one international peer-reviewed journal. She is a member of Asian Media and Information Centre (AMIC), Association of Business Communicators in India (ABCI), Public Relations Society of India (PRSI), Indian Society of Training and Development (ISTD), and is a regional coordinator of Society for Management and Behavioural Sciences.

Her areas of interest include corporate communication and responsible business activity.

INTRODUCTION

Ahmedabad based Boddhi Power Transmission Ltd (BPTL) - a part of the diversified Boddhi Group based in Mumbai, forged a strategic alliance with Ahmedabad based SGC Projects Ltd, under which it acquired 40.5% shares of SGC Projects Ltd at USD 0.80 per share from the existing promoters. BPTL is part of the Boddhi group, promoted by Navya Bharadwaj. It is based in Mumbai and has been operating primarily in the real estate industry for the past 35 years. With a turnover of over USD 150 million, the group also has interests in international trading, office stationery etc. The USD 25 million SGC Projects Ltd. is a civil construction company undertaking infrastructure projects and holds orders in hand worth USD 45 million. BPTL is a USD 55 million public listed company that builds power transmission lines and has executed projects for Power Grid Corporation of India, State Electricity Boards and overseas projects based in Mumbai. BPTL stated on the alliance, "The ultimate objective of alliance is to make SGC a subsidiary of BPTL, and along with the existing promoters, control the company. The proposal was approved at the board meeting of both companies. The day to day operational management of SGC Projects will continue to run under the leadership of managing director, Sarvesh Sharma. The alliance of SGC and BPTL would entail tremendous growth opportunities, given the rapid growth in the infrastructure and civil engineering construction sector."

ORGANIZATION BACKGROUND

Company Profile – SGC

SGC projects Ltd. (SGC) is a leading player in the civil construction of buildings and industrial structures, and infrastructure projects such as roads and bridges. It is a public limited company based in Ahmedabad and is promoted by Sarvesh Sharma and Kushagra Gaur.

SGC was incorporated on June 25, 1986 as Avon Construction Private Ltd. Subsequently the name was changed to Sharma & Gaur Construction Private Ltd. in January, 1989; and to SGC Projects Private Ltd. on January 20, 1995. It was then converted into a Private Ltd. company on March 14, 1995 under the name SGC Projects Ltd. The company entered the field of industrial construction with the prime motive of servicing reputed clients with very high quality of construction work. The company has achieved substantial growth and is one of the leading construction companies in Gujarat. It has been registered as a class 'A' contractor with Government of Gujarat. SGC is one of the construction companies certified under ISO 9001:2000 quality management system by TUV Management Services of Germany. The company is mainly engaged in the construction of industrial and residential buildings and also power and infrastructure development projects. SGC has to its credit many prestigious projects in the industrial, power, institutional and infrastructure sectors, and is acknowledged as a reliable and professional construction company by the discerning and quality conscious market.

SGC's building construction includes the construction of residential complexes and townships, hospitals, hotels and commercial complexes. The company has also worked on various civil infrastructure development projects like construction of roads, bridges and terminals. SGC Mining & Quarries is a wholly-owned subsidiary of the company.

Regional Offices of SGC are located in Bangalore, Delhi, Kolkata and Mumbai. Mumbai office is the SGC's Corporate Office, while the registered Office is in Ahmedabad, being the founding city of the company.

Company Profile – BPTL

BPTL was incorporated on May 5, 1981 as RT Power Structure Private Ltd. and became a public company on November 18, 1993. Its name was changed to its present name on February 15, 1994. BPTL is a leading global engineering, procurement and construction (EPC) player with diversified interests. It is mainly engaged in the business of power transmission and distribution sector, including design and engineering, procurement, fabrication, erection, installation and construction, testing and commissioning, post commissioning operation and maintenance. BPTL is also engaged in oil & gas pipeline and railways' EPC business and infrastructure development projects. It has its presence across more than 40 countries globally. It was the first Indian company to be ISO 9001 certified in the transmission industry.

SETTING THE STAGE

Change in management Control

A MOU (Memorandum of Understanding) between SGC group Directors, their relatives and Goyal Investments and Finance Pvt. Ltd. ("Sellers") and Boddhi Power Transmission Ltd. and Boddhi Energy Pvt. Ltd. ("Purchaser") was signed on September 11, 2004 for purchase of Equity Shares of SGC constituting 34.28% of the paid up capital of SGC. Pursuant to the said MOU, a public announcement was made on September 12, 2004 by the Purchaser to acquire 25% (11,61,638 Equity Shares) of the share capital of SGC from the existing shareholders of SGC pursuant to Regulations 10 & 12 of SEBI (SAST) Regulations, 1997 on account of proposed substantial acquisition of equity shares and change in control of SGC.

A Share Purchase Agreement was entered into between the aforesaid parties on September 28, 2004 for purchase of 1,500,000 Equity Shares at USD 0.80 each, representing 34.28% of the share capital of SGC. Boddhi Energy Private Ltd. which was one of the Purchasers in the SPA, relinquished and surrendered all their rights, powers and claims in relation to the operation of SGC. By virtue of the above transaction, the promoters of SGC are Mr. Sharma and Mr. Gaur. SGC became the subsidiary of BPTL w.e.f. March 5, 2007.

"The SGC management will remain the same and this step is a strategic move to develop synergies between the two companies," declared the joint spokesperson.

SGC's Work Culture

SGC believes in delivering quality without any malpractices. There had been a continuous growth in the profits of the organization. With the growth of the organization, there had been a change in organizational structure and organizational policies as well. Till the year 1999, there were no functional departments and a single person used to handle several departments.

Redeployment of the employees

The company believed in replicating the organizational culture to all its offices. When the company started expanding, they started their office in

Udaipur and shifted a senior officer from Ahmedabad to Udaipur. Post this, Administrative head, Operational head & Finance head & few coordinators were transferred to the new office in Udaipur. The Director supervised this closely and would go there every week to take ensure a smooth transition. There was another project of a car factory which was initiated at Gurgaon, and since it was a large project, again some key employees were shifted from Ahmedabad to Gurgaon.

SGC'S Human Resource Philosophy

SGC's most valuable assets are its employees. To match the pace with global competition, the company believes in equipping their employees to be effective, efficient and responsible; by providing quality education and opportunity to develop and improve their skills. The training is largely need-based with experienced mentors to guide the employees, working towards increasing the productivity and placing them in the forefront of technology advancements.

SGC also believes in robust recruitment process. SGC is committed to finding the best talent to lead their business in a competitive environment. The company intends to provide the 'Right Person for the Right Job' and tries to find the right candidate by effectively mobilizing resources.

Employee Orientation

Discussing the employee-centric approach of SGC before the alliance with BPTL, the ex-VP (HR) shared, "SGC has the best salary structure in the industry, which was as per income tax format and hence lessened the tax burden. Other Human Resource policies like leave and travel policy are also employee friendly and among the best in the industry. Leaves can be accumulated, increasing convenience for employees. The company believes in continuous learning and development of its employees. Hence the Training and Development function is given due importance and training is a regular feature. There is no hire and fire policy."

CASE DESCRIPTION

In 2003 the company bagged the biggest project ever in Udaipur on a subcontracting model. The contracting policies were rigid and difficult. There was a hike in raw material price by 50-60%, and since the project undertaken had strict terms and conditions, there was no change in the contractual amount. Since SGC could not increase the contractual amount, they had to incur a heavy loss. Besides this, SGC worked on credit, and repayment by clients was an area of concern. This lead to a disruption in cash flow due to which SGC had to borrow from different financial institutions. Hence, interest burden increased and after some time the financial institutions were reluctant to give further loans. The clients' money was outstanding and it started affecting the operations of the company. This meant that the raw material for operational requirement was procured on credit.

Looking at the financial state of the company, the vendors decided to give the products on credit at a higher rate. The plight was that the client would not share the burden of higher credit rates to the company, and hence did not increase the contract value. Despite these problems, the salary of the employees were given on time. The money from clients could not be recovered though and the company moved into arbitration and subsequently into court cases.

BPTL and SGC Alliance

SGC made huge losses in the year 2008. Hence it had to be restructured. Since the financial health of SGC was deteriorating and the credits were outstanding, SGC had to plan and ensure financial viability. Hence a decision was taken to complete the alliance with BPTL. The stocks of the promoters of SGC were bought by BPTL in September, 2006, and BPTL took over SGC. Ethical values of BPTL and SGC matched and hence there were no major differences in employee policies. Initially BPTL was involved only in financial decision and later in procurement, but it never involved in the operational decisions. The alliance started a power division. But the power industry was not doing well, and high overhead costs reduced profitability. Alliance of BPTL & SGC completely made sense in terms of synergy. BPTL is into power transmission i.e. electrical infrastructure. A part of it is also construction and deals with public boards and government. So their liaising and business processes are similar. The main interests of the Boddhi group is into housing and buildings. It also relates to construction. SGC was into housing, as well as power stations, huge buildings for public use, roads and factories etc. Hence this was a horizontal diversification for BPTL. Moreover the headquarters of BPTL and SGC were in Ahmedabad, making movement for meetings logistically easier.

Around 2002-2004, One of the SGC's project did not fare well and ran into losses, and had to be rescued. That is when BPTL bought a stake in SGC. SGC was a not a big player till then. With BPTL's involvement, its revenues increased. BPTL infused the funding and bank guarantees that are required in undertaking such projects in the EPC industry. SGC was in liquidity crunch, whereas BPTL was financially very sound. SGC was very sound technically, and was strong in industrial and real estate, whereas BPTL was very sound in commercial projects. BPTL had a very strong reputation in the market and could get money from the market very easily which could be a very strong point for SGC. As both the companies together could make a perfect organization, and SGC with the help of BPTL could come out of the liquidity crunch, an alliance was decided.

It was perceived that since Boddhi group and SGC would have conflict of interest, hence it was decided to make SGC a subsidiary of BPTL, keeping BPTL autonomous from the Boddhi Group.

SGC got trapped into a scam where government institutions were also involved and hence the offices of SGC were raided. After raids and enquiries, SGC Ahmedabad office was closed down as this division was responsible for all that construction scam. The Ahmedabad office acted as their headquarter, but it was also a regional office of one of the divisions viz. Buildings and Factories. Roads and Infrastructure division was always based in Mumbai, while the Power and Railways division was in Delhi. The major problems were confronted by Buildings and Factories division which was alleged in the scam and was also suffering major losses because of recession. In addition to this, it was directly competing with Boddhi group in some markets (like Mumbai residential building industry market). It was therefore decided to close the Ahmedabad office, merge the resources and leverage on the synergy.

BPTL since its inception is headquartered at Mumbai. The top management including the Chairman, Managing Director, and board of directors were placed at the headquarters in Mumbai.

A senior Human Resource professional who had been with SGC for more than a decade narrated the incident and experience of shifting base. He said "One of the business unit head left SGC (Ahmedabad) after eight years of working. At that time, to manage the situation BPTL decided to shift to Mumbai. There was a huge client base in Mumbai. MNCs were establishing themselves in that region. BPTL decided to appoint a western head in Mumbai. Infrastructure division already had its head office in Mumbai. Hence, the shift to Mumbai started. They forced some of the employees to move to Mumbai. Many of them were working for last 10-15 years, and hence due to different reasons like education of children, job of the spouse, and comfort in the city etc. the employees did not want to shift the base. But the company left them with only two options - either move to Mumbai or leave the company. Consequentially many employees choose to leave."

As BPTL has its corporate Office in Mumbai, the BPTL Management started to take decisions which were earlier under the scope of the SGC Management. The decisions were not taken in confidence with the promoters of SGC. Due to these discrepancies, one of the promoters Mr. Sharma also left.

CASE DISCUSSION

Corporate operations were transferred to Mumbai office. The employees from various departments were also shifted to Mumbai – Plants & Machinery, Operation, R&D, Procurements and Finance. Again, with the introduction of this change, many of the employees left the company. This affected the morale of the employees who stayed, and there was survivor's syndrome, that there can be further such transfers of the team members.

Infrastructure and Power division had problems. There was organizational restructuring, and hence the organizational structure also changed. The different regional offices were merged. Power and Northern India Infrastructure Division have been merged and now have operate from Punjab. Now there were corporate team members. The head would report to corporate team members and site members would report to regional heads. With the removal of the heads or moving away from the place, the site members were affected and they were not been able to adjust as these new heads could not understand the culture of the organization. Profitability reduced and Human Resource policies also changed. This affected the morale of the employees. The performance appraisal system was changed and Key Result Areas (KRAs) and performance related salary were introduced. Leave policy also changed.

The GM (HR), reflecting upon the changes in the employee policies, discussed about the issues in the implementation of these changes stating, "At times things are not in the control of supervisor and the slowing down of the work is due to the change in Government policy. At times even the work is slowed down on the request of client and hence supervisors are forced to underperform. This would affect their performance appraisal. Due to performance linked pay structures, the supervisor's pay would be adversely affected due to their underperformance. If the project is not progressing, a purchase manager cannot do anything. Due to external factors the management has decided to move slowly due to clients' receivables. So, it would be against performance based pay. Despite the fact that the factors were not under the control of the site members or supervisors, they have to bear the brunt. This affected the morale of the employees."

There was a fear of unknown among the employees and this made transition difficult. There were many employees who were working for more than 15 years. These employees found it a bit difficult to cope up with the change and thus were always under the fear of insecurity. Shifting to Mumbai with their families was really getting difficult for them. Some employees voluntarily accepted to shift to Mumbai where as some were forced to. Those who did not want to shift resigned and left the company. Other than these problems, it was an amicable and transparent alliance. Other than the shift to Mumbai, the culture, environment and leadership of the company was not so drastically changed.

BPTL's management and leadership style was not very different from SGC and employees of SGC never faced any kind of problems as far as salary, increment and working pattern and style is concerned.

Difference in Culture

The culture of the two organizations looked similar superficially, but there were some drastic differences between the two. The Manager - HR, who had been the employee of SGC as well as BPTL confessed, "Culture wise they were very different. BPTL came from a high profit, less competitive industry. Moreover it was operating in a highly specialised sector. Hence the attrition rate was very low. This also led to high bureaucracy. Moreover the industry is very traditional with little innovation. Hence need of training did not exist. SGC was in a competitive industry. Moreover the management team was highly educated and promoted meritocracy. They had strong people processes in place and they realised that success of every project depended purely on their people, and less on technology."

A similar sentiment was shared by Ms. Kapadia, who joined SGC as an intern and later served as a full-time employee at SGC for eight years. She said, "BPTL was a conservative company and more of family driven culture. There was no focus on training and development activities and Human Resource activities were very limited whereas SGC was highly system driven. A lot of focus was on training and development of employees. Human Resource activities at SGC were extremely organized and the company was more employee centric."

Difference in Human Resource Architecture

The difference in the Human Resource Architecture at both the allies is noticeable. Mr. Patel, who has witnessed this alliance and has worked with SGC before and after the alliance, summarizing the difference in the role of Human Resource department in both the organizations, quips that "The focus on how the people department was set up was different right from the beginning. SGC hired regularly from campus. They promoted fresh blood and also young people. BPTL hardly used to have campus placements. Also because of a difference in rate of attrition the strategy was different. Moreover, none of the BPTL competitors had an office in the same state. Hence the attrition rate at HQ was negligible. On projects, the attrition rate was similar, but BPTL had fewer highly skilled team members and more semi-skilled contract employees while SGC had an equal ratio of both. Thus, training was needed and properly set up and implemented at SGC. BPTL does not have properly designed training. Increments and promotions were merit based at SGC whereas at BPTL it was primarily on basis of tenure.

The functional departments like production, design and construction worked in silos without coordination with Human Resource Department, and hence Human Resource was more of a staff function at BPTL. But at SGC, Human Resource was more of a line function and other functional departments worked in coordination with Human Resource Department than in SGC."

Appointment of the New Directors

One of the promoters Mr. Sharma resigned from the Board. The new alliance decided to restructure the Board of Management and appointed new directors whom they managed to poach from their competitors. The new Directors pulled few more of their team members from their ex-employers. This started affecting the culture of the organization and the employees did not appreciate it and were apprehensive about the fairness and justice of this action. Mr. Shah and few of his other colleagues quoted, "One of the new directors who joined had a culture and value system very different, and they have affected the original culture in a negative way. The environment present earlier was of 'freedom and trust' which has been replaced by 'control and fear.' This affected the employees, and led to distrust. The employees do not enjoy autonomy and would not take decisions. One of the new functional heads has brought others from his previous workplace where he worked for 25 years. All these new hires are for key positions. The new Director is not system driven but person driven."

Some of the employees added, "Induction process is not handled properly and the new joinees are not inducted to the ethos of SGC. The SGC culture is lost in this transition. The new system has affected not only the existing employees but also the new joinees. Overall, the employees are uncomfortable. Both the older and new members are also leaving the organization. Employee productivity has decreased. Inter departmental issues have increased."

One of the senior professionals stated irritably, "The new purchase head and new plant and machinery head were hired despite the fact that the plant and machinery head were already there for around four years, and there was no need of a new recruit. But the fact was that the new hire was given due consideration as the Director wanted team members from his previous organization to join SGC. Hence, both the heads were asked to head the plant and machinery division and there was no role distribution amongst them. Slowly and gradually, power shifted from the older head to the new appointee, and the older one was asked to leave." The employees found that the transparency of SGC was clouded under a garb of ambiguity and communication gap.

Due to organizational restructuring, new regional heads were appointed. Site members found it difficult to adapt as the new appointees were not inducted to SGC's culture. Due to this, there were issues between regional level and site level managers as they have different orientations. The site managers, who have been working for years, were forced to prove their mettle again. Around 75% key project members resigned from Ahmedabad office. As they were to report to regional Project Manager who was stationed in Mumbai, the project members in Ahmedabad were distressed and they left. All these issues led to the higher turnover of employees not only at Ahmedabad Office but also at Mumbai office. Those who relocated to Mumbai are also leaving the company to take up new jobs as the opportunities increased with the boom in the industry and they have better opportunities.

CONCLUSION

The organization decided to bring in some interventions to control the situation. They introduced activities for team building at project level so that the new team members gets accepted by the older ones, and everyone gets to know each other. They hired an external consultant to help the company out of this crisis. The consultants realized that due to change in the line of leadership, a leadership survey must be conducted, and hence a survey was conducted first for top management and then for middle level managers.

Top management was also put through team building activities where all four SBU (Strategic Business Unit) heads and functional heads (corporate heads) participated in three programmes which were scheduled for two days every month. This helped them know each other better, as they were new, and also helped them identify their leadership style and team behaviour.

The company's culture and value are deviating and employee centric organization has changed its policies ruthlessly. The change in management has not turned out to be very positive.

WORK OR LIFE:
THE RIGHT BALANCE

AUTHOR BIO

Dr. Ritu Sharma

Dr. Sharma is currently engaged as an Assistant Professor and Head of Department, Psychology with Pandit Deendayal Petroleum University (PDPU) Gandhinagar. Dr. Sharma is a gold medallist, and holds a Ph.D. in Psychology. She has over 12 years of work experience in teaching, training and research; and is involved and effective in the complete gamut of academic activities – teaching, research and institutional development. Dr. Sharma is engaged with international and national research projects and training assignments in the areas of human behaviour, personality development and psychometric profiling. She has conducted several workshops and training programmes for the academia, corporate and NGOs in various areas of human behaviour and interpersonal effectiveness.

She has lectured extensively on various topics related to Application of Psychology in Industry and Society in national institutes. Currently she is also a project head from India for a study on "Women's Economic Empowerment in Asia: Psychosocial and Anthropological factors". She has widely published papers in journals of national and international repute. She has presented papers in several international and national level conferences both in India and overseas; and has represented university research work in various institutes in Europe and Australia. She is an Associate Life Member of Indian Association of Clinical Psychology. She is Member of Confederation of Indian Industry (Western Region), Indian Women Network (IWN) and International Economics Development and Research Center (IEDRC). She has been nominated as an Executive Council Member of Indian Association of Cognitive Behaviour Therapy, and as Board of studies members for two other Universities in Gujarat.

Dr. Ruchi Tewari

Dr. Tewari is engaged as a Faculty, General Management, with over 18 years of academic and industry experience. She has worked in the area of General Management, exploring the Communication of Corporate Social Responsibility (CSR) for her Doctorate in Philosophy (Ph.D.); which she completed after an M.Phil. in English. She has done extensive research work in the area of CSR and has worked on various aspects of applied communication. Her professional horizon encompasses teaching communication and development related courses and guiding post-graduate students, presenting and publishing research papers in national and international conferences and journals, conducting trainings, completing projects and consultancy assignment for organizations.

She is an established trainer associated with several organizations in Ahmedabad where she conducts regular sessions as a part of the employee development programmes organized by them. She has conducted over 500 hours of training in various organizations like telecommunication (product and services), manufacturing, real estate and education.

Dr. Tewari has 20 publications in national and international academic journals and several chapters in edited books. She has also presented 15 conference papers in national and international conferences. She is an editorial review member for two national and one international peer-reviewed journal. She is a member of Asian Media and Information Centre (AMIC), Association of Business Communicators in India (ABCI), Public Relations Society of India (PRSI), Indian Society of Training and Development (ISTD), and is a regional coordinator of Society for Management and Behavioural Sciences.

Her areas of interest include corporate communication and responsible business activity.

EXECUTIVE SUMMARY

The Kapoor couple had a flourishing career in the software sector. They had a three year old son and an infant daughter. They were highly aspirational, and the organizational human resource policies of their organization had a huge impact on their future.

Before moving to R. K. Infotech at Chennai, they had been in Japan where their employers had offered them immense support and help in managing their personal lives along with performing their duties effectively. The current case details the different work-life balance strategies adopted by people-friendly organizations around the globe and the implications of these policies. The case also brings out the role and impact of work life balance in effective organizational performance.

SETTING THE STAGE

Rajat and Shahana were deliberating over an important decision. Taking care of two children – a three year old son and an infant daughter – with full-time jobs was proving a challenge. Therefore one of them would need to move to a different organization, which might result in a compromise on professional growth and other benefits offered by the new organization, which might be lower than the current organization. The added worry was that there was no social or family support which they could expect because their marriage was against the wishes of their respective families.

They were presently posted in Chennai, working at R.K. Infotech. Prior to this they had worked in Japan. Working in Chennai posed numerous issues such as cultural differences. Language barrier was a bigger barrier than they felt in Tokyo. Due to this several issues arose, such as inability to find day-care and school for their infant daughter and son respectively.

CASE DESCRIPTION

Both were alumnus from a premier engineering college of the country. After marriage they managed to get their first job in SoftTank Inc., a Japanese company, and moved to Tokyo. SoftTank Inc. is ranked among the Top 10 employee friendly companies in Japan. The company reflected firm faith in corporate social responsibility (CSR). Ensuring Work-Life Balance (WLB) for its employees was SoftTanks's immediate expression of its conviction in CSR.

Their son Samir's birth had complications but being in Tokyo the couple seemed well supported because SoftTank Inc. offered immensely supportive environment for women welfare and childcare privileges. Its policies were in accordance to the "The Work-Life Balance, 2008, Charter of the Government of Japan (Government of Japan, 2008)" which recognizes the need for work life balance amongst the Japanese employees and therefore calls for action stating, "To enable various kinds of care and community participation, as well as to respect the needs of individuals for personal time to live healthy, happy lives, Japanese society must diversify its work options."

They received childbirth allowance of USD 6,000. Flexible work arrangement was given to Shahana comprising of flexible-time and job-share along with reduced working hours. "Kids leave" was sanctioned to the couple for four weeks and Shahana was granted an extended paid leave of another four weeks. In addition, a discounted homemaking service was offered where 20% discount was offered on house cleaning and 25% discount for other services like laundry, car washing and cooking. The child-rearing supportive portal was a great aid in child-rearing. The portal gave an easy access to a panel of doctors with whom Shahana and Rajat could resolve their queries and anxieties. SoftTank Inc. also organized lectures and workshops for male employees aimed at sensitizing them to the emotional and physical needs of a new mother, stress, nutrition and safety etc. They helped male employees by organizing cooking classes and the childrearing support handbook '医療 (Iryō)' meaning *Care* for managers acted as a comprehensive guide to understand the various company policies and terms for employees with children. The sensitivity which Rajat developed due to the culture prevalent at SoftTank helped the couple cope up with the new familial situation. The day cares and crèches at SoftTank gave Shahana the confidence to get back to work because she was allowed to take breaks from work. Rajat was granted 'Summer Hours' so that he put in some extra time on weekends ensuring that he could head out early on Friday and spend time with his family.

On March 11, 2011, a massive earthquake struck Japan. The couple decided to move back to the home land because Rajat felt very insecure leaving six month pregnant Shahana and two year old Samir. He constantly dreaded his inability to protect his family in case of another recurrence of any calamity.

The couple decided to move back to India. The first offer they got was from an Information and Technology (IT) company in Mumbai. They moved back to India and worked for three months. Unfortunately they were asked to re-locate to the headquarters in Chennai. In August 2011 the family including their children – two and a half year old Samir and three month old Rihanna moved to Chennai.

Working in India posed numerous challenges. There was a dearth of professionally managed services for childcare. Work hours were also erratic. Rajat often found himself working over weekends to meet deadlines. Between work pressure and responsibility of raising their kids, they found no time to socialize. Relatives and friends advised that Rajat should continue with the full-time employment and Shahana should concentrate on needs of the family and take care of home. The young couple could not take this option since their expense were high and could not be met with a single source of income.

Both Rajat and Shahana regretted their decision of getting back to India, wondering if it was judicious. They were unsure whether they were in an organization which did not offer such benefits, or if it was rampant across other organizations too. Connecting to their parents and reconciling with them seemed the only possible option to them.

CASE DISCUSSION

Work-life balance strategies which organizations adopt will help build a positive and constructive environment where both professional as well as family life is taken care of.

Government Role to Play in Charting Policies of WLB

The boom in the Indian economy has made a strong case for work-life balance in India. The Indian workforce is in greater stress than counterparts in developed nations. A large rise in percentage of working women has also added to the complexity. The Maternity Benefit Act of 1961 requires that a three month paid leave be given to all women workers. The Factories Act (1948) requires the employer to provide a crèche if there are more than 30 women employees with children below six years. The Sixth Pay Commission (2008) has clarified the child care leave in respect of central government employees.

It would facilitate women employees to take care of their children at the time of need. The Maternity leave has been increased from the period of 135 days to 180 days by the Sixth Pay Commission. The Maternity Benefit Act 1956 entitles every woman liable for the payment of the maternity benefit at the rate of average daily wage for the period of her actual absence and the period following the date of delivery. The Factories Act, 1948 directs that a factory in which ten, or more than ten workers are working, should concentrate on the health and welfare of the workers working in the factories. Crèche facility is required if there are more than thirty women with children below six years. A trained female staff is be to appointed in charge and milk and refreshments for the children are provided. Women workers have to be given period intervals to feed the kids.

The weekly hours should not be more than 48 hours a week where the first day of the week shall be a weekly holiday, or one of the days three days before or after the said first day. The Amendment Act bill was passed in 2005 where women workers were prohibited to work in night shift and there would be no change of shift after a weekly holiday or any other holiday.

Analysis Can Be Done Keeping Following Perspectives in Mind

This case highlights the issues relevant to working couples in present time. The current work scenario is marked by fast pace of change, intense pressure, constant declines, changing demographics, increased use of technology, and coexisting virtual workplace. Juxtaposed with this, the increase in average income and rise in living standards have individuals striving for better work atmosphere. (Shankar & Bhatanagar, 2010). Work-life balance has implications for employee attitudes, behaviours, wellbeing as well as organizational effectiveness (Eby *et al.*, 2007).

Family Friendly Initiatives to Resolve Work-Life Interfaces

Today, women make up 40% of the global workforce. They are a part of the shift seen worldwide from agricultural work to formal workforce in the industry and service sector jobs. Family-friendly policies can help women employees to balance work and family responsibilities; yield benefits for themselves, for their families, and their employers. The Family-Friendly Workplace (FFW) Model is best applied to companies that make a substantial investment in training employees and/or must comply with national or international employment standards. With greater urbanization and a shift of working preference in the formal sector, the demand for companies to provide family-friendly benefits is likely to grow. The FFW Model helps businesses to easily analyze the relative costs and rewards of offering family-friendly benefits. Using the model enables businesses to reap the potential cost savings of family-friendly policies and contribute to improved health for employees, their families, and the broader community.

Formal Organizational Initiatives

To frame formal work-life balance initiatives is the need of hour for the organizations and Human Resource professionals. In countries in Asia Pacific, concerns include rural migration to urban areas, gender inequality in remuneration and lack of career development. These socio-demographic changes place pressure on firms to be proactive in addressing issues concerning work-life balance, including the provision of Family Friendly Workplace arrangements (Hall & Liddicoat, 2005).

Creating Family Friendly Supportive Work Culture

As cited by Deepak Chawla & Neena Sondhi (2011), the more 'Supportive' organizations shape an implicit psychological contract (Rousseau 1995) between the organization and the individual. This aids and enhances his work/non work conflict and at the same time increases an individual's sense of commitment.

Personal Values, Beliefs and Life Style for Work-Life Enrichment

Values, worker type, role demand and conflict are some of the elements that domain has emphasized. In the second discourse, research has focused on family friendly policies offered by organizations including flexible work arrangement. (Shankar & Bhatnagar, 2010).

Spirituality and Work-Life

A large volume of research shows that people who are more religious and spiritual have better mental health and adapt more quickly to health problems compared to those who are less religious and spiritual. These possible benefits to mental health and well-being have physiological consequences that impact physical health, affect the risk of disease, and influence response to treatment. (Koenig, 2012) confirms in his study that increased spirituality was positively associated with increased well-being, increased sense of meaning and purpose in life, and decreased tendency to become angry.

CONCLUSION

Work-Life Balance (hereinafter WLB) is a much broader concept requiring attention of working individuals at large, whether or not they are married, and whether or not they have family obligations. Intensification of work and technology that blurs the boundary between work and personal life provides challenges for everyone. Competitive and customer pressures have forced companies to rationalize and restructure, and as a consequence less people have to do more work. WLB should not only refer to a balance between work and family, but also between work and the other personal activities. It is an all-encompassing issue pertinent for business to consider.

REFERENCES

Casper, Wendy J., Eby, Lillian T., Bordeaux, Christopher; Lockwood, Angie; Lambert, Dawn (2007). A review of research methods in IO/OB work-family research. *Journal of Applied Psychology*, 92(1), 28-43.

Chawla, D., Sondhi, N. (2011). Assessing Work-Life Balance among Indian Women Professionals, *Indian Journal of Industrial Relations*, 47(2), 341-352.

Government of Japan. (2008). Work-life Balance Charter (In Japanese). Retrieved October 13, 2016, from http://www8.cao.go.jp/wlb/government/20barrier_html/20html/charter.html

Hall, L., Liddicoat, L. (2005). Challenges to Developing Effective Family Friendly Work Practices: Findings from New Zealand, *Research and Practice in Human Resource Management*, 13(1), 1-17.

Koenig, H.G. (2012). Religion, Spirituality and Health: The Research and Clinical Implications, *ISRN Psychiatry*, 2012, Article ID 278730, 33 pages.

Shankar, T., Bhatnagar, J. (2010). Work-Life Balance, Employee Engagement, Emotional Consonance/ Dissonance & Turnover Intention, *The Indian Journal of Industrial Relations*, 46(1), 74-87.

SECTION

STARTUPS AND ENTREPRENEURSHIP

Overcoming The Hurdles: An Example Of Systematic Feasibility Study Of A New Startup In Singapore

Author Bio

Ms Phyu Thwe Hnin

Phyu Thwe Hnin is an MBA graduate from Northampton University. She is also a member of Association of Chartered Certified Accountant (ACCA). She was born in Southern Shan State of Myanmar, a city name called "Kalaw". She is presently working in Singapore as an Accounts Executive with Tat Hong Metals Pte Ltd, where she is responsible for handling the entire function of accounting activities. Her ambition is to become a successful female entrepreneur based on work-life balance.

SUMMARY

The purpose of this case study is to highlight the common problems a startup faces which contributes to the high failure rate. In order to discuss viable solutions, a new business (Ili translator) is used. The case shows how Ili tackled and overcame the hurdles faced such as understanding of entrepreneurial attributes, unique product proposition, market research, industry analysis, technical feasibility study, financial feasibility study, scenario planning, and scalability study of the venture. Although 90% of the new startups have a potential to fail, this study verified that it is possible to be successful when the shortcomings are identified and resolved.

BACKGROUND

In the twenty-first century, businesses are facing numerous challenges. In order to cope with a complex, demanding and ever-changing market; creating a new business venture with a new product, or penetrating into a new market has become a popular business strategy for companies and entrepreneurs. Nonetheless, in doing so, most of the competitors end up doing similar businesses with the same method (Rowen, 2008) which results in potential failures. Hence, implementing innovative business venture has become the main critical success factors to gain competitive advantages in the market and ensure organization's continuous survival. This is particularly true in city-state Singapore. Although it is a well-known startup hub, it has prominent weaknesses such as a small market yet extremely costly business ecosystem. Unofficial data shows that 50% to 70% of new startups fail within the first 18 months due to the entrepreneur's half-heartedness, lack of applied innovation advantage, lack of marketability, incompetent management style, and most importantly absence of detailed planning.

Drucker (1985) mentions that innovation is an important tool in entrepreneurship because both innovation and entrepreneurship demand creativity. In pursuing objective of implementation new business venture, many entrepreneurs realized that the key to success is based on performing opportunity analysis or feasibility study (Stevens et al., 2006). Opportunity analysis is the process of analyzing the nature of opportunities available in the environment of the new venture. Gofton (1997) notes that conducting feasibility study is an effective way to safeguard minimum wastage of resources for investment.

Consequently, this study exemplifies the problems a new business venture faces, and the viable solutions that Ili ensured in the following eight areas, namely attributes of the entrepreneur, value proposition of the new venture, market research, industry analysis, technical feasibility study, financial feasibility study, scenario planning, and the scalability study.

CASE DESCRIPTION

The success of any business depends on the founder/s. Without the right attributes, the leaders will lack the ability to lead the organisation to success (Business News Daily, 2016). Entrepreneurs are widely known as individuals who have the ability to evaluate business opportunities, gather necessary resource, utilize them effectively, and initiate appropriate action to ensure success (Meredith et al., 1991). Generally speaking, entrepreneurs are achievement-oriented, and they like to take responsibility of making critical business decisions. According to Manfred (1997), entrepreneurs are frequently regarded as the key drivers in an enterprise, and as motivational leader capable of getting the best out of people. Additionally, Hood and Young (1993) note some areas of business skills that are crucial to entrepreneurial achievements which include leadership skills, communication skills, human relationship skills, management skills, negotiation skills, analytical thinking skills, decision-making skills, goal setting skills, and business plan preparation skills.

The differences in the skill set between an entrepreneur and a manager lie in the ability to identify business opportunities and implement the new venture. As indicated in Exhibit 1, Timmons (1989) mentions that a successful entrepreneur must have the creativity and innovation of an inventor, and the business management skills of a manager. As an entrepreneur, it is necessary to acquire a basic understanding and knowledge of fundamental business areas such as finance, marketing and sales (Hood &Young, 1993).

Exhibit 1: Entrepreneur – More Than an Owner/Manager

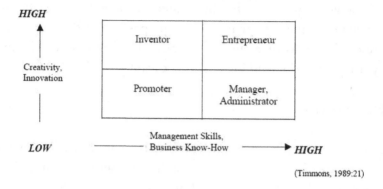

FIGURE 1: ENTREPRENEUR – MORE THAN AN OWNER/MANAGER

(Timmons, 1989:21)

Source: Timmons, 1989

Consequently, before embarking in their startup journeys, entrepreneurs could use various forms of aptitude tests or seek professional Human Resource practitioner's advice to determine whether they possess the ability of entrepreneur in terms of skill, attitude, and business knowledge. For the purpose of this case study, the author took reference from Sánchez's model (2012) together with other models such as McClelland's need theory and Maslow theory to assess, and determine entrepreneur's behaviours as shown in Exhibit 2.

Exhibit 2: Entrepreneurial Motives and Behaviours

Factors	Rating
1. Needs for overcome a challenge and personal growth (Need for success)	High
2. Motivation of money (Professional autonomy)	Medium
3. Need for personal autonomy (Self-employment); Need for more flexibility in personal life	High

4. Need for affiliation & institutional power; Contribute to the welfare of the community	High
5. Ego need, need to feel important; Gain respect & social admiration	Medium
6. Need for competition; Exploiting business opportunity	High

Source: Authors

Furthermore, the entrepreneurship specific human capital also includes entrepreneurial capability, parental background and attitudes, while the venture specific human capital includes knowledge of the domain and motivations (UNCTAD, 2008). Based on these named areas of analysis, Exhibit 3 affirms that the author possesses the characters to be a competent entrepreneur.

Exhibit 3: The Entrepreneurship Specific Human Capital

Human capital	Characteristics	Rating
General	Education	High
	Managerial human capital	High
	Capabilities	High
	Demographic control variables	Medium
Entrepreneurship specific	Entrepreneurial capability	Medium
	Parental background	Medium
	Attitudes	High
Venture specific	Knowledge of the domain	High
	Motivations	High

Source: Authors

Venture Description and Value Proposition

Skok (2016) states that product problems is one of the five reasons why startup fails. To attain an innovative product advantage, the new venture must have a compelling value proposition (Anderson, Narus & Van Rossum, 2006). In this study, the proposed product is a portable Translator – Ili. This is the world's first wearable translator designed for travellers that work across English, Chinese and Japanese. The translator is similar to the size of a pendant, and users can wear around their necks like an iPod (Staff, 2016). To attain applied innovation, Ili must deliver values and experiences that exceed travellers' expectations (London, Pogue & Spinuzzi, 2015). In this aspect, the first value proposition of Ili is to overcome the language barrier and to encourage communication. It enables travellers to go places where they may encounter unfamiliar local language (Logbar, 2015). It is a real-time translator that works without Wi-Fi, 3G, or any other internet connection.

Additionally, in a more macro view, it could improve the travel and tourism industry in Singapore. In 2014, Travel & Tourism generated USD 66 billion of Singapore's Gross Domestic Product (GDP) which is more than twice as large as the retail sector. Skok (2016) concludes that a successful product must meet the market needs; therefore, Ili is targeting the travel-related business where it can help to build relationships and create various networks in hotels, local governments, retail stores, car rental business, amusement parks, transportation and travel agencies to expand its market.

Case Discussion

Market Research

Patel (2016) has determined 'lack of a market need for a company's product' as the single biggest reason for startup failure. Different markets have different characteristics and expectations. Market research allows the entrepreneurs to understand their targeted market and how the market will react to their products or service before they are distributed to the market (Van Den & Joshi, 2007). Market research is essential for every business, and it must be conducted on a continual basis in order to cope with changing market trends and to achieve competitive advantage. Regardless of implementing a new business or expanding the existing one, market research will promote understanding of the target market and its nature.

In order to analyze the market characteristics of translator Ili product, the marketing mix (4Ps) was derived. Palmer (2004) mentions that 4Ps can be used to implement both long-term corporate strategy and short-term tactical plan. As shown in Exhibit 4, in the process of analysing the respective 'Ps' of Ili's marketing mix, the corresponding market strategies were determined.

Exhibit 4: Marketing Mix for Ili

Marketing Mix (4P)	Target	Examples of Market Strategy
Product	Ili	The focus should be on the product differentiation as Ili is the very first portable translator that does not need any internet connection. The high quality microphone and speakers generate a clear and loud translated message. Travellers can easily communicate with the locals and create wonderful memories.
Place	Travel and tourism Sector	There is e-commerce website for online purchasing that has worldwide delivery. As a distribution network, travel agencies, hotels and rental store will be the main target.
Price	Competitive pricing	Will offer a value-for-money product with a reasonable price. The price range will be from USD 100–USD 200 which is considered competitive for an innovative product.
Promotion	Discounted travel packages and accommodation offer	Attractive discounted travel package and accommodation arrangement will be offered from the local travel agency for every purchase of Ili product.

Source: Authors

In addition, a Buyer Intention Survey was conducted based on 100 frequent travellers. Young working executives were selected for this survey. As per the survey (see Exhibit 5), more than 80% of travellers are willing to buy Ili within the price range of USD 150-USD 200. Singapore purchasing demands are based on online purchasing primarily on buying travel tickets and electronic gadgets. 77% of travellers' first language is English, and 90% of the travellers prefer to use English. Among them, 73% of travellers want to travel Japan, China, and French. The survey results verified the marketability of Ili in Singapore market.

Exhibit 5: Buying Intention Survey

Survey Question	Answer
Q1. How frequently did you travel last year?	
a. None	3 %
b. Once a year	56%
c. Twice a year	27%
d. Three times and above	14%
Q2. How do you usually buy travel tickets?	
a. From travel agent	31%
b. At the airport	13%
c. Online	49%
d. None of the above	7%
Q3.How many language/s do you speak?	
a. 1	21%
b. 2	56%
c. 3	23%
d. 4 and above	0%
Q4. Is English your first language?	
a. Yes	77%
b. No	23%

Q5. Which language are you most interested in apart from English?	
a. Chinese	23%
b. Japanese	34%
c. French	13%
d. Thai	8%
e. Korean	12%
f. None of the above	10%

Q6. Which country would you like to travel the most?	
a. Japan	32%
b. China	20%
c. Africa	3%
d. French	21%
e. Australia	10%
f. None of the above	14%

Q7. When you travel, how do you communicate with locals if they don't speak English, or when you are unfamiliar with their language?	
a. By translator (or) guide	55%
b. By dictionary	28%
c. By Google translate	10%
d. None of the above	7%

Q8. How do you prefer to shop for electronic gadgets?	
a. Online	52%
b. Convenience shop	32%
c. Directly from manufacturer	16%

Q9. Are you interested to buy a wearable translator without using the Internet? 　　a.　Yes 　　b.　No 　　c.　Maybe	 88% 7% 5%
Q10. How would you rate the price range for a wearable translator for USD 150 to USD 200? 　　a.　Reasonable 　　b.　Expensive	 87% 13%

Source: Authors

Industry Analysis

Lack of understanding of the industry will certainly contribute to the startup failure. According to Entrepreneur (2016), the ultimate aim of conducting an industrial analysis is to gain an understanding of the relative strength of competitors. In this context, Ili will be distributed in Singapore as a sole distributor by targeting the travel and tourism industry. As Ili is an innovative product and there is no direct competitor in the market to date, it possesses a competitive advantage. However, with reference to Michael Porter's Five Forces analysis, Google translate and e-dictionary are substitutes of Ili. Among these products, Ili's cutting edge technology in terms of fast translation process, ability to operate without an internet connection and two-way communication process makes it a preferred-product.

In 2014, Singapore's travel and tourism industry has been growing faster than other economic sectors such as automotive industry, financial service industry and healthcare industry etc. (WTTC, 2015). In order to analyze the attractiveness of IT gadget industry, Porter's Five Forces analysis was conducted. Five Forces analysis is a powerful method to analyze the industrial attractiveness based on the threat of five factors: customer, supplier, existing competitor, new entrance and substitute (Porter, 1998). As indicate in Exhibit 6, the bargaining power of supplier is high, the threat of new entrant is medium, and ot her three factors of bargaining power of customer, threat of competitive rivalry and threat of substitute product are low. Hence, it can be concluded that IT gadget industry is an attractive industry for Ili to be marketed in Singapore.

Exhibit 6: Porter's Five Forces Analysis on IT Gadget Industry

Forces	Description	Level of Threat
Threat of competitive rivalry	In the current market, there is no direct competitor for Ili product as it is an new innovation	Low
Bargaining power of customer	In the current market, Ili is a new and innovative product with no direct competitors who can provide the same features. Hence the bargaining power of customer will be low.	Low
Threat of substitute product	Google translate and E-dictionary are Ili's substitutes. However Ili offers some features of competitiveness over its market.	Low
Threat of new entrant	As the company is marketing Ili under the arrangement of sole distributorship in Singapore, the company has a competitive advantage. However, other innovative translator gadgets may be imported into the market. The initial setup cost of such company will vary according to the product range.	Medium

Bargaining power of supplier	As the company is just merely distributing Ili in the market, and is importing it from Japan; bargaining power of the supplier is strong. Additionally, for future software update, the company will have to depend totally on the manufacturer.	High

Source: Authors

Technical Feasibility Study

Technical feasibility study refers to the detailing of project requirements that are necessary to complete the project and testing how much the project will be able to satisfy customers (Nagarajan, 2004) without which a startup will face potential failure.

As the main product of Ili will be imported from Logbar Inc. of Japan, there are varied technical expertise that will be required to ensure quality control and inspection (Zurich, 2011). An expert technical team will be assigned to inspect and accept the goods imported from Japan. If there are notable defects or damages, the company will inform Japan headquarter directly for further actions. As the product is an electronic gadget, it is essential to have a few service centres in Singapore which will support the customer in case of a technical problems and warranty related issues. For the after-sale service of Ili product, another expert technical team will be in charge. It is necessary to have a workshop to perform inspection and repair of any software technical requirement. The spare part/s of aftersales service will be stored in the warehouse. To implement an E-commerce website for Ili, in-house or outsourced software developers are needed. For the effective usage of online ordering function and marketing, employees need to have proper training of social media marketing. Ili will be patented based on the targeted travel and tourism industry, where its main target customers are travellers. This will ensure that it complies with legal formalities.

The technical analysis revealed that the Ili product idea has the potential to be successful as the company has considered the various technical aspects which are important to the target customers. This will boost customer confidence in the product and in turn increase the demand for the product.

Financial Feasibility Study

To avoid the downfall of a new business venture, it must be financially viable. The economic return generated from business to investors must be equal, or higher than the return on investment that investors initially capitalized. Estimated income generated and estimated cost of operation and administration charges are essential in considering the financial feasibility of the business (Bennet, 2003). A financial feasibility study is a useful tool used to analyse the financial viability of a business. It consists of analyzing the performance and financial position of a business and forecasting for next five years. Furthermore, the decision is based on estimated return and risk and financial feasibility study evaluates risk and return (Fabozzi & Peterson, 2003).

As per the estimated financial performance of Ili for the next five year, the business displayed a potential of success even at the introductory stage (see Exhibit 7). Nevertheless, capital infusion is needed for most of the new startup business in the introductory stage. According to the projected financial performance, in order to achieve the estimated revenue, heavy investment in marketing expense from 2016 will be expected as the product is in the introductory stage in Singapore market. The overall financial performance of Ili is healthy and it can be concluded that this new venture is financially feasible to market.

SCENARIO VERSIONS

Detailed scenario planning will enable a startup to remain adaptable in turbulent business environment as they will be equipped with dynamic capability in formulating respective contingency plans (Phadnis et al., 2015).

For first five years after introducing Ili product in Singapore, the following scenario versions and possible actions have been considered in order to cope with emergencies and unforeseen circumstances.

1. What if a product with similar functions is launched in Singapore?

Different foreign markets will be identified and strategic penetration into the new markets will be implemented in order to gain competitive advantage over the competitors.

2. What if there is insufficient initial capital for business startup?
    In this case, the inventory level and target sales unit will be reduced until the business can generate the additional and sufficient revenue.

3. What if any other company offers an acquisition bid?
    Acquisition will only be considered after five years of operation.

4. What if there is difficulty in getting qualified engineers / technicians from the market?
    The company will provide effective training package for every engineer / technician and personal development training with the support offered by the supplier.

5. What if there are more technological advanced features of translators launched in the market?
    The company will continuously conduct research and development on the fundamental product for more advanced functions according to market demands. Continuous update will be offered to every Ili user.

6. What if the company does not meet the estimated sales level?
    The company will invest in marketing and promotional functions, and aim to improve sales figures by taking advantages of social media marketing techniques.

Scalability of the New Venture

Menasce (2000) states that scalability has a connection with the performance of the new venture. It encourages the growth of a venture while preserving the consistency of operation, culture, and profitability. Hallowell (2001) confirms the necessity of knowing the scalability of the business venture as the business needs to serve a large number of additional customers at minimum incremental cost. In the scalability concept, there are two approaches to pursue organizational growth (Agrawal et al., 2011). The first method is to scale up where only one function of the business will be modified by adding more resources. The second method is scale out, which has an implication on the whole business by adding more resources to the all business verticals. Once the scalability plan is established, business can be assured of an increase in sales and profits, without a huge impact on other factors. In order to implement it, the business needs to have a business plan, require human resources and technical support.

CONCLUSION

This case study highlights the problems and offers solutions in eight common areas a startup faces in order to avoid potential failure. It presents the necessity of a systematic opportunity analysis to evaluate the innovative market of the electronic gadget sector, especially for a wearable translator, based on the related factors in Singapore travel and tourism industry. It was illustrated that this feasibility study could lower the risk of startup failure. Due to Ili's innovative product idea, it is necessary to perform feasibility study to realize whether the business idea fits into the targeted travel and tourism industry in Singapore, which is expanding continuously, and has proven to be an attractive industry according to Porter's Five Forces analysis. The existing travel and tourism industry is volatile and complex, and always demands creativity and innovative product and services. According to the feasibility study conducted, Ili faces a high level of challenge in the market as the bargaining power of supplier is high, and its business idea can be easily replicated by other companies and entrepreneurs.

To summarize, the case study illustrates the implementation of feasibility study in a new venture, to increase the level of success. Based on self-analysis, product proposition study, market research, industry feasibility study, technical feasibility study, financial feasibility study, scenario planning and scalability study, it can be concluded that a new startup such as Ili wearable translator can be successful in the chosen market.

REFERENCES

Anderson, J.C., Narus, J.A., and Van Rossum, W. (2006). Customer Value Propositions in Business Markets, *Harvard business review*. 84(3), 90

Agrawal, D., Abbadi, A.E., Das, S., and Elmore A, J. (2011). Database Scalability, Elasticity, and Autonomy in the Cloud, *Lecture Notes in Computer Science*. 6587, 2-15

Bennett, F.L. (2003*). The Management of Construction: A Project Life Cycle Approach.* Burlington: Butterworth-Heinemann

Business News Daily (2016). *Leadership Failures: 5 Stumbling Blocks for Bosses.* Retrieved October 14, 2016, from http://www.businessnewsdaily.com/7293-why-leaders-fail.html

Entrepreneur (2016). *Competitive Analysis: How Will Your Business Compete? Explain It Well in Your Business Plan's Competitive Analysis.* Retrieved October 25, 2016, from https://www.entrepreneur.com/article/25756

Fabozzi, F.J. and Peterson, P.P. (2003). *Financial Management & Analysis.* 2nd ed. New Jersey: John Wiley & Sons.

Gofton, L. (1997) *Business Market Research.* London: Kogan Page

Hallowell, R. (2001). Scalability: The Paradox of Human Resources in E-Commerce. *International Journal of Service Industry Management,* 12(1), 34–43.

Hood, J. and Young, J. (1993). Entrepreneurship's Requisite Areas of Development: A Survey of Top Executives in Successful Entrepreneurial Firms, *Journal of Business Venturing.* 8(2), 115-136.

Logbar (2015). Wearable Translator, *Logbar Inc.* Retrieved October 30, 2016, from http://www.iamili.com/.

London, N., Pogue, G., and Spinuzzi, C. (2015). Understanding the Value Proposition as a Co-Created Claim, *IEEE International Professional Communication Conference (IPCC).* 1-8.

Menasce, D.A. (2000). Scaling for e-business. *Proceedings 8th International Symposium on Modeling, Analysis and Simulation of Computer and Telecommunication Systems,* 511–513.

Meredith, G.G., Nelson, R.E. and Neck, R.A. (1991). *The Practice of Entrepreneurship.* Lagos: University Press.

Nagarajan, K. (2004). *Project Management.* New Age International.

Patel, N. (2016). *90% Of Startups Fail: Here's What You Need To Know About The 10%.* Retrieved October 9, 2016, from http://www.forbes.com/sites/neilpatel/2015/01/16/90-of-startups-will-fail-heres-what-you-need-to-know-about-the-10/#4f00723755e1.

Phadnis, S., Caplice, C., Sheffi, Y., and Singh, M. (2015). Effect of Scenario Planning on Field Experts' Judgment of Long-range Investment Decisions, *Strategic Management Journal,* 36(9), 1401-1411.

Porter, M.E. (1998). *Competitive strategy: Techniques for Analysing Industries and Competitors; With a New Introduction.* New York: Simon & Schuster Adult Publishing Group.

Rowen, H.S. (2008). *Behind East Asian growth: The Political and Social Foundations of Prosperity.* London: Routledge.

Skok, D. (2016). *5 Reasons Why Startup Fails.* Retrieved October 14, 2016, from http://www.forentrepreneurs.com/why-startups-fail/.

Staff Writer (2016). Wearable translator Ili works without WiFi. *The Strait Times.* Retrieved October 25, 2016, from http://www.straitstimes.com/world/united-states/wearable-translator-ili-works-without-wi-fi.

Stevens, R.E., Sherwood, P.K., Dunn, J.P. and Dunn, P.J. (2006). *Market Opportunity Analysis: Text and Cases.* New York: Best Business Books.

Timmons, J.A. (1989). *The Entrepreneurial Mind.* Andover Massachusetts: Brick House Publishing Company.

UNCTAD (2008). *Promoting and Sustaining SMEs Clusters and Networks for Development.* Geneva: United Nations Conference on Trade and Development.

WTTC (2015). WTTC Travel & Tourism Economic Impact 2015. *World Travel & Tourism Council.* Retrieved September 14, 2016, from https://www.wttc.org//media/files/reports/economic%20impact%20research/regional%202015/world2015.pdf.

Van Den Bulte, C., and Joshi, Y.V., (2007). New Product Diffusion with Influential and Imitators, *Marketing Science,* 26(3), 400-404.

Zurich (2011). The Technology of iIspection. *Zurich Engineering.* Retrieved October 14, 2016, from https://www.zurich.co.uk/internet/home/SiteCollectionDocuments/Engineering/thetechnologyofinspection.pdf.

FROM PAYMENT GATEWAY TO E-WALLET – THE JOURNEY OF PAYTM

AUTHOR BIO

Smita Dayal

Smita has an MBA degree (dual specialization in finance and marketing) with a brief stint in the banking industry in the area of branch banking and loaning to small and medium enterprises. She completed her B.Com (Honours) from SRCC, Delhi University. Being academically inclined, she continued in the education field both as a Ph.D. student and a lecturer. She cleared UGC NET in management and joined Mithibai College as an Assistant Professor. She was later appointed as a coordinator of B.Com in banking and insurance department of K.J. Somaiya college of Arts and Commerce where her profile included coordination work, as well as planning and execution of live projects, industrial visits, arranging for guest lectures and other academic and non- academic activities. Currently she is a full time faculty in Banarsidas Chandiwala Institute of Professional Studies, an Indraprastha University affiliated college. Her research interests include consumer behaviour and strategy. She has published several academic papers in national as well as international journals of repute.

ORGANIZATION BACKGROUND

Paytm was founded by Vijay Shekhar Sharma in 2000 and incubated by One97 Communications in 2010 as a prepaid mobile recharge website. Paytm is an acronym for "Pay through Mobile" with Android, Windows and iOS applications.

Paytm is one of those companies which have evolved over a relatively short span of time. They transitioned from payment gateway to e-commerce to wallet and now are about to launch as a payment bank. Paytm started off by offering mobile recharge and utility bill payments and today offers a full marketplace to consumers on its mobile application. They have over 100 million registered users, and in a short span of time have scaled up to more than 60 million orders per month.

Funding

Paytm is the consumer brand of mobile internet company One97 Communications. One97 investors include Ant Financial (AliPay), SAIF Partners, Sapphire Venture and Silicon Valley Bank. In March 2015, Indian industrialist Ratan Tata made a personal investment in the firm. The same month, the company received a USD 575 million investment from Chinese ecommerce company Alibaba Group after Ant Financial Services Group, an Alibaba Group affiliate, took 25% stake in One97 as part of a strategic agreement. Paytm borrowed USD 50 million from ICICI Bank in March 2016 as working capital. By January 2016, Paytm had already received approximately USD 1.5 billion, excluding the working capital loan of USD 50 million. The current valuation of Paytm is approximately USD 4 billion.

Paytm Business Model

Paytm began operations as a payment gateway, but is now an e- commerce website, an online wallet, and is now transforming into a full-fledged payment bank. Their business includes mobile recharge, online bill payments, e-commerce and wallet, movie ticket booking, air, rail and bus ticket booking, hotel booking, etc.

Paytm delivery channels include:

1. Website
2. Mobile Website
3. Mobile Application (Android or iOS or others)
4. Affiliate networks (Bloggers, Coupon Websites, Review Websites etc.)

The various revenue lines of Paytm include:

1. **Web Portal**: E-Commerce i.e. they earn from commissions received from listed sellers on total sales.
2. **Listing Fee and Convenience Fee:** Sellers are charged listing fee for selling on Paytm and on-boarding fee for doorstep service of explaining everything related to selling online.
3. **OTA Bookings:** Paytm recently ventured into Online Travel Agency Model (OTA) where it is providing air, bus etc. ticketing and hotel booking and thus earning commissions on transactions.
4. **Payments Integration:** Paytm wallet can be used to pay all sorts of utility bills including cable, internet, mobile, gas, electricity etc. They earn a commission from the utility providers.
5. **Mobile Wallet:** Integrating its wallet across major e-commerce and e-payment enabled online sellers (replaces a traditional payment gateway with the exact same business model but lower fee and Transaction Discounting Rates (TDR)). The balance of the wallet is deposited by Paytm to generate interest income.
6. **Transaction revenue model:** Paytm charges 4% commission if you transfer your wallet balance to your bank account.
7. **Advertising Revenue model:** Paytm allows sellers to promote themselves through advertisement on Paytm website. The sellers need to pay a certain charge to avail this facility.
8. **Data:** By selling data they collect from smart phones.

Paytm Marketplace

The shopping market is working at the click of a mouse, thereby transforming the e-commerce place into a big globe for shopaholics. The marketplace of Paytm is like a usual e-commerce website shopping environment. They offer a wide range of categories to pick from. There are various shopping verticals relating to business to consumer (B2C) selling: electronics, men's fashion, women's fashion, home and kitchen, sports, health and beauty, automotive store, baby, kids and toys, gifts and sweets, books, stationery, industrial supplies (tools, spare parts, lab supplies, machines etc.). Paytm also offers Business to Business (B2B) selling in the form of a wholesale vertical.

Paytm offers discounts on MRP (Maximum Retail Price) and in addition offers cashback on nearly all its products. There is also "Paytm Bazaar" which offers limited period deals to customers. To avail the cashback offer all a customer needs to do is apply the promotional code. Other services like doorstep delivery, return facility, easy and secure payments, tracking of shipment etc. add to the overall shopping experience.

Listing Fee

The listing fee refers to the percentage of commission that Paytm charges the firms. This varies depending on the category of product that Paytm sells. It ranges anywhere between 0% to 20% of the sale value (excluding taxes and discounts).

Let us assume customers A, B & C Purchase five products from Paytm - a book, a stereo, a fridge, a mobile phone and a bed sheet from three sellers. Total pay-out by Paytm and receipts look. Exhibit 1 shows how the final receipts and total pay-out by Paytm are recorded in Paytm's books of accounts.

Exhibit 1: Snapshot of Paytm Commission Model

S. No.	Item Name	Price USD)	Taxes (Assume Flat 10%)	Total Price	Seller Name	Product's Commission %	Service Tax	Paytm's commission	Total received by Paytm	Total received by Seller
Col A	Col B	Col C	Col C * 10%	Col D	Col E	Col F	Col G	Col H = Col F * Col C	Col I = Col H * (1+Col G)	Col D - Col I
1	Book	8	50	58	Seller A	15%	14.50%	1	1.37	56.63
2	Stereo	15	100	115	Seller B	8%	14.50%	1	1.37	113.63
3	Fridge	300	2000	2300	Seller B	8%	14.50%	24	27.48	2272.52
4	Mobile	600	4000	4600	Seller B	6%	14.50%	36	41.22	4558.78
5	Bed Sheet	15	80	95	Seller C	20%	14.50%	3	3.44	91.57

Source: Authors

The total of Column I (USD 74.88) is the total revenue of Paytm from sale of goods. This is one of the basic revenue models for Paytm.

Ota Bookings

Paytm allows online travel booking for cars, bikes, bus, railways, airlines, hotels, movies etc. All of these generate revenue through a commission based model. Paytm witnessed 3,000 bus bookings on the first day of launch of the facility in 2012. Paytm entered a market which is dominated by the likes of Redbus, Makemytrip, etc., but with a feature of cashback facility it has created differentiation. For hotel bookings Paytm has partnered with players such as Goibibo, Ezeego and TSI-Yatra. Paytm has caused a lot of disruption in the travel space, and is in talks with Booking.com and Expedia.com for partnering with them to include international hotels in its inventory.

Paytm allows the users to book rail tickets directly via IRCTC direct on the Paytm platform. According to the Paytm Vice President Mr Abhishek Rajan,

"Our alliance with IRCTC is a major leap as it completes the spectrum of air, road and rail ticket booking solutions available on Paytm. This is a significant milestone in our efforts to build India's largest travel marketplace."

Payments Integration

Paytm offers a comprehensive experience to the customer. A customer can recharge mobile (both prepaid and post-paid) and landline, pay utility bills like electricity, water, gas, recharge metro cards, DTH recharge, broadband bill pay, insurance premium, and water bills. Cashback option generates savings on recharge and utility bill payment.

Online recharge is just 5% of USD 15 billion recharge market. Paytm leads this increasing online recharge segment. 30% of the online recharge is done by Paytm. It earns commission from the utility bill companies or telecommunication companies. There is also a time difference between collections of the payments by Paytm and remittance to the firms, allowing Paytm to earn an interest on the collections from the bank during the interim.

Paytm has recently tied up with Jugnoo – an auto rickshaw aggregator firm launched in 2014, allowing auto rickshaw drivers to recharge the customer's Paytm wallet. This addressed the issue of returning change after completion of the ride. This offers immense convenience to customers. This option would also provide the auto-rickshaw drivers with access to instant cash that will be deducted from their revenue generated from Jugnoo app. There is a feature on the app that enables drivers to initiate the recharge by inputting the customer's phone number. The customers receive a confirmation message on their phone as soon as the recharge process is initiated by the driver. Once the customers agree to the confirmation notification sent to them, the recharge is processed.

Mumbai and Delhi metro commuters can also recharge their metro smart cards using the Paytm application via the official websites. While Government entities may not entertain commissions to Paytm, they surely link the customer to Paytm's wallet since Paytm gives cashback on all of these in the form of wallet cash, which can only be redeemed against a payment made via its network.

Mobile Wallets

A wallet is pre-paid financial instrument, which allows its customers to store money in a 'virtual wallet'. The money kept in a virtual wallet is in effect stored in an escrow account of the wallet service provider with a bank and, on average, generates interest income comparable to those of fixed deposits. However, the interest income is not passed on to the customer nor does it figure as the primary revenue source for the wallet company. Its revenue accrues from the commission paid by the merchants, whose transactions are conducted by people using the wallet. Similar to credit cards, it is a mode of payment and it charges commission which ranges between 1-2 % of the transaction value. Paytm wallet works exactly like the payment gateways of other e-retailers, discounting the value of the transaction by 1-3% and giving the rest to the merchant. Thus payment wallets make money the exact same way as payment gateways do, with an additional stream of income by keeping money stored on a unique customer ID (phone number, email id etc.) and earning an interest on that. Out of the payments made by the customer, the seller gets the discounted revenue after deducting the transaction fee charged by Paytm.

The money in the Paytm wallet does not lie idle but is deposited by Paytm in a flexi-deposit allowing Paytm to earn approximately 7.5% interest rate on the amount deposited, along with a facility to withdraw the amount any time in accordance to the customer withdrawals. This helps Paytm earn huge amount of money eg. Even a wallet balance of USD 50 from 10,000 customers make a total deposit pool of USD 500,000. This translates into a significant amount of money, considering the pan-India customer base of Paytm.

Paytm Strategy

The strategy that Paytm uses is not merely a promotional strategy but a cleverly designed customer acquisition strategy. Customers are not looking out for television advertisements but they are more allured towards discounts and cashbacks. Paytm is trying to attract new customers by giving cashback (not discounts) on MRP. Customers in India are not clear about margins on MRP. There is a high margin on branded as well non-branded products. The cashback goes into the Paytm (mobile) wallet of the customer which forces him to reuse Paytm and buy more and in turn Paytm retain its customer. Thus, a circle of purchase, cashback and repurchase continues. This aids in continuance of buying behaviour on Paytm, creating a pool of loyal customers. Paytm also partners with other major sites where wallet money can be used for transaction.

The main purpose of giving a cashback to the customer is to create stickiness. At the same time, the concept is used to play with the human mind that likes the idea of receiving extra while spending the same amount of money. When customers use wallets to make payments, Paytm passes on a certain percentage of the transaction fee earned back to the customer as cashback.

Paytm is moving towards becoming a small online bank. They are encouraging customers to pay via Paytm money. In their ads it is clear that "Paytm Karo" is the core business for them. So when customers buy from Paytm, the refund money would be Paytm money. The Paytm money can be utilised only on Paytm and hence, the customer has an incentive to stay. Paytm can share a percentage (or full) of the transaction fee earned from sellers with the customers as cashback. This will not only help them acquire a rich pool of the customers but also wipe out small competitors who cannot sustain the discounts and cashback offered by Paytm. They suffer huge losses or lose out customers who are extremely price sensitive. Paytm has strong backing from the likes of Alibaba to withstand initial losses. In future they will fine-tune their business strategies to start earning profits. Paytm had been operating for quite some time under the radar much before any of their competitors even existed. So they have had a first mover advantage. They are well funded, and have expanded their product line from being a recharge depot to a shopping site.

Paytm has now got an in-principle licence from Reserve Bank of India to become a payment bank. Paytm will be transforming into a bank once all the requirements are met. Paytm will launch its net banking and debit cards soon. They are planning to capture untapped rural market in India where banking has not yet reached.

ANALYSIS

Conjoint analysis was done on a sample of 35 individuals who have prior experience of using an e-wallet. The objective was to find out the relative importance of the attributes of Paytm. The following attributes, as shown in Exhibit 2, were identified from literature review to test their relative importance to a customer:

Exhibit 2: Attributes Impacting Satisfaction with Paytm

Attributes	Levels
Cashback facility	Yes / No
Utility bill payment facility	Yes / No
Shopping facility	Yes / No
Facility to store money in the wallet	Yes / No
Data security	Yes / No
Option to transfer money to other accounts	Yes / No
Payment alternatives	Debit Card and Credit Card / NEFT / COD

Source: Authors

Exhibit 3 shows the test results and the relative importance of different attributes.

Exhibit 3: Conjoint Analysis Test Report

Attribute	Relative Importance
Cash_Back_Faccility	18.25%
Utility_bill_payment	4.77%
Shopping	10.59%
Store_money_in_wallet	13.24%
Discounted_price	4.40%
Data_Security	2.29%

Transfer_money	7.96%
Payment_alternatives	38.50%

Source: Authors

As per the findings, the most important attribute for Paytm customers is the availability of alternative payment options followed by the cashback facility. The customers also prefer an e-wallet which also offers option of e-commerce i.e. the option of shopping. The facility to store money in the e-wallet is the next best attribute. Paytm should therefore offer alternative payment platforms and continue to give the cashback facility and shopping options on its website or mobile application.

A customer faces several trade-offs while selecting the best e-commerce website. Conjoint analysis is a statistical technique that helps the marketer understand the combination of attributes that is most preferred by the customer. In this particular study the researcher proposed eight attributes where seven of them had two levels - Yes or No; and only one attribute had three levels – Debit / Credit Cards, NEFT and COD (cash on delivery payment option). The statistical technique helped identify the best and the worst combination of the eight attributes and their levels. This is shown in Exhibit 4.

Exhibit 4: Best and Worst Combinations of Attributes

Best Profile	**Worst Profile**	**Attribute**	
Yes	No	Cash_Back_Faccility	
No	Yes	Utility_bill_payment	
Yes	No	Shopping	
Yes	No	Store_money_in_wallet	
Yes	No	Discounted_price	
Yes	No	Data_Security	
No	Yes	Transfer_money	
COD	NEFT	Payment_alternatives	
Part-Worths			
Feature	**Levels (Part-Worths)**		

Cash_Back_Faccility	Yes	No	
	0.63	-0.63	
Utility_bill_payment	Yes	No	
	-0.16	0.16	
Shopping	Yes	No	
	0.36	-0.36	
Store_money_in_wallet	Yes	No	
	0.45	-0.45	
Discounted_price	Yes	No	
	0.15	-0.15	
Data_Security	Yes	No	
	0.08	-0.08	
Transfer_money	Yes	No	
	-0.27	0.27	
Payment_alternatives	Debit / Credit Card	NEFT	COD
	0.39	-1.52	1.12

Source: Authors

It was identified that the combination of attributes and their levels that is most preferred by the customers is availability of cashback facility, shopping on the website, facility to store money in the e-wallet, discounted prices, data security and availability of cash on delivery as a payment alternative. Thus, not giving much importance to utility bill payment facility and the option to transfer money to other accounts.

Paytm is a preferred brand compared to its e-wallet competitors like Citrus Pay. Mobikwik, Pockets, PayU Money because it not only offers all the features of an e-wallet, but also offers shopping across various product categories in addition to offering cashback facility.

CONCLUSION

Paytm is growing rapidly and is expected to strengthen its offerings even further post its launch as a payment bank. Paytm's strong funding and customer acquisition as well as retention strategy will further fuel its growth. Paytm is slowly emerging as a household name and people use it in one form of the other, whether as an ecommerce platform, a recharge facility, booking platform or a payment gateway. It offers the whole gamut of facilities under a single umbrella and is therefore increasingly preferred by customers as their go-to option.

Taxi And Auto Aggregators: Disrupting Traditional Transport

Author Bio

Anshita Agarwal

Anshita has worked with NIIT Technologies Pvt Ltd in the airline domain as a software developer. She has nearly two years of experience working in agile methodology. As a software developer, she has been responsible for interacting with clients and creating high level and low level design for the user stories decided, followed by coding, testing and merging the code created.

Anshita has completed B.Tech in Computer Science from Teerthankar Mahaveer University (College of Engineering), and is currently pursuing an MBA in Human Resource Management from Amity Business School Noida. She won the third prize for a case study presented at "Conduit" Case Study competition organized by Amity Business School.

Executive Summary

In the last few years auto and taxi aggregator services have gained immense popularity in India. These companies include are Ola, Uber, Jugnoo etc. They have fleets of cabs and autos, and other on-road services. These aggregators consider themselves as technology companies, and are excluded from the transport regulations which other transport operator have to follow. These aggregators have the ability to match supply and demand successfully with the help of technology. Smartphone proliferation and disruptive technologies have made these companies a hit among users. These companies have intelligently addressed the gaps within the traditional taxi systems and created a win-win situation for drivers, cab operators and customers. This paper attempts to study how these companies have impacted lives of people and disrupted the traditional transport system in India.

Setting The Stage

Even though there were many taxi providers and auto service providers – there was a sense of monopoly as they operated with their own self-serving guidelines. Taxi drivers often have the tendency to bargain with passengers over unjustified fares and cause inconvenience to the customers. This has been a problem, and the customer need for a reliable cab service was so far untapped. There was a huge gap between demand and supply of cabs and autos. The emergence of technology changed the face of the taxi and auto service sector.

Industry Background

In pre-aggregator-era taxis were provided by car agencies. In cases of high demand, cab availability would be severely compromised and waiting times would increase substantially. Moreover there was no precise information about the driver, there was lack of security in the cab, and high prices were common. Smartphone proliferation and increase in Internet use not only enabled these aggregators to be become successful, but also enabled customers to get a cab conveniently. In fact, this worked as the trigger for the companies to go app-only from an earlier model of a call and book centre.

Timeline

Mega Cabs and Fast Track Taxi started in 2001 with small fleets. The market, however, started seeing traction only from 2006 onwards when the likes of disruptors such as Meru Cabs, Easy Cabs and Savaari emerged. There are now several players in the fray.

During Phase 1 of the industry, companies owned fully owned fleets, with the drivers as salaried employees Bookings were done over phone calls. Due to this model, the companies had to incur high capital costs, take car loans, pay EMI, take care of high maintenance costs etc. There were also recurring strikes by the drivers that affected the service. During Phase 2 of the industry, companies either registered cars owned by small fleet owners, or those of single car owners, after doing full verification. Using this, model companies incurred low capital expenditure and maintenance cost. The current phase is a hybrid model in which part of the fleet of cars or autos are owned by companies. This helps companies provide quality service and incur low cost.

Taxi space (market) in India has seen a phenomenal growth in the past few years. A large amount of venture capital (VC) is being infused in the sector. The biggest player in the taxi aggregator space is Ola cabs which has recently acquired Taxi for Sure. Its biggest competitor in the taxi space is Uber. Jugnoo, which is an auto aggregator, competes with Ola in the auto market. These taxi aggregator companies neither own cars nor employ drivers; they simply connect users with drivers using technology. They do not follow an inventory-driven marketplace, but rather a technology-driven one.

ANALYSIS

The research finding as shown in Exhibit 1 shows the constant increase in the number of Internet users over the years.

Exhibit 1: Increase in Users of App-Based Car Services

Year	No. of user in Millions
2012	48
2013	91
2014	137
2015	238
2016	371

Source: IAMAI

Discussions were held with drivers in Delhi-NCR region, and it was verified that these aggregators are using hybrid business model. The industry continues to grow, with Ola and Uber capturing most of the market share. Customers are increasingly opting for these services as an alternative to self-driving / public transport. A comparison of traditional transport facilities against services provided by aggregators is shown in Exhibit 2.

Exhibit 2: Changes from Traditional To Current Aggregators

Activity	Traditional Transport System	Services by Aggregators
Price	Price hikes, No fixed rates	Companies have fixed rates for each segment of cars.
Security	Lack of safety measures; the rides were not traceable.	Ride booked through these aggregators apps are traceable
Information	No information about the driver or car	Complete information about the car and driver available.

Punctuality	Lack of punctuality maintained by the driver during pickups or drops.	There is punctuality maintained by the driver during pickups or drops. This is recorded by the companies.
Feedback Mechanism	Feeble feedback mechanism to answer to complaints on driver behavior or any other issues.	Quick actions are taken on complaints by customers.

Source: Authors

Impact on Ecosystem

1. Drivers viewpoint

- Has brought new drivers to the ecosystem
- Drivers get monthly salary ranging from USD 300 to USD 600 per month.
- Drivers who own their vehicles can earn around USD 800 per month.
- The lives of traditional taxi drivers lives has been impacted
  a. Some drivers have joined these aggregators.
  b. Some unions are against it, especially in Delhi and Karnataka.

2. Customers viewpoint

- Traditional services and cab operators are improving their own services in face of the competition.
- Customers have a number of choices at their disposal.
- Feedback mechanism and safety measures is one of the biggest factors that customers have always wanted, and aggregators have provided.

Conclusion: Action Plan And The Way Forward

There are various other parameters that impact aggregators and their efforts to scale up and disrupt the transportation system. Programs should ensure that customers are interested in the services, and use them more frequently. This can be done by giving customized offers and enhanced services. Reaching out and increasing penetration in Tier II and Tier III cities will be the next big goal.

Unfortunately, current policies and guidelines are unclear on several finer points. Price surge (which raises prices exponentially during peak hours) is still a tricky proposition and needs to be addressed in a way that ensures all stakeholder's participation. Since there are no clear cut guidelines, the entire sector falls into a grey legal area. The government needs to ensure that no one takes an advantage of the situation, and that the taxi drivers do not suffer. The government, along with various stakeholders need to establish schemes for the traditional cab or auto drivers to evolve in this new technology-intensive ecosystem.

WOMEN'S AVENUE –
CASE STUDY OF A
SUCCESSFUL SOCIAL ENTREPRENEUR

AUTHOR BIO

Dhruv Jain

Dhruv Jain is currently pursuing her degree in business management at Vivekananda Institute of Professional Studies, Guru Govind University. He has worked as an intern in an export firm. Dhruv is also involved in various societies in his college and holds a position of head coordinator in marketing society (Mark-e-xpress, VIPS) and research and development society (Anveshan, VIPS) at his college. He is working in an NGO named "The Saviours" and has organised several events such as blood donations camps and awareness drives as the event leader.

Tanya Bansal

Tanya is currently pursuing her degree in business management at Vivekananda Institute of Professional Studies, Guru Govind University. She is a part of the marketing society and has represented her college in various competitions and events at Delhi University. She has done several virtual internships in social media promotion and content development. She is also pursuing an additional course in Digital marketing from 'Delhi School of Digital Marketing.'

Harsmita Bhatheja

Harsmita is currently pursuing her degree in business management at Vivekananda Institute of Professional Studies, Guru Govind University. She has experience of working in virtual internships as a cluster manager. She has a strong interest in debating and has represented her college in various debate competitions. She is an active member of the marketing society of her college.

Mayank Gandhi

Mayank is currently pursuing her degree in business management at Vivekananda Institute of Professional Studies, Guru Govind University. He has experience in content writing. He also has experience of working as a cluster manager and digital marketing head. He has a strong interest in emerging markets and startups. He has also represented his school in an inter-state Psychology Olympiad in 2014.

INTRODUCTION

Social entrepreneurship is aimed at benefit of society where the entrepreneur is also the promoter and works for the welfare and upliftment of society by taking on financial risks, but with a hope of earning profits. Social entrepreneurs are those individuals who have innovative solutions to society's most pressing social problems. They are ambitious and persistent, tackling major social issues and offering new ideas for wide-scale change.

Women are increasingly intervening into the domain of social entrepreneurship. There are also numerous examples which showcase women working towards social causes and providing a platform to those women who are inflicted and suffering due to various reasons. Women Entrepreneurs may be defined as the woman or a group of women who initiate, organize and operate a business enterprise. A sense towards independent decision-making in their life and career is the motivational factor behind this urge. Women entrepreneurship is recognised as an important source of economic growth. Women entrepreneurs provide society with different solutions to management, organisation and business problems by creating new jobs. However, they still represent a minority of all entrepreneurs and their potential is underutilized.

Despite all the social hurdles, success stories of women emerging in India can be seen frequently. Women as entrepreneurs are becoming social innovators and empowering other women and girls from society. Women leaders are self-confident, persuasive and willing to take risks. Their ability to learn quickly from her persuasiveness, open style of problem solving, willingness to take risks, ability to motivate people, knowing how to win and lose gracefully are the strengths of Indian women entrepreneurs.

SETTING THE STAGE

Meera Kumar was a girl from Delhi who was living a routine life with her parents. Her father was a renowned businessman. The young girl was pursuing her graduation from Delhi University. Sohan, who was Meera's driver, used to drop and pick her up from the college. One day, in a state of inebriation, Sohan took Meera to a secluded place and molested her. She was later abandoned on the road. She was helped by some samaritans and was brought to the hospital in a critical condition. Her physical rehabilitation took two months, but she continued to face a mental trauma.

She finally decided to forget about her ordeal and look to her future. She decided to help other victims too who had faced such ordeals. She decided to pursue her interest in the culinary industry, but was daunted by the challenge since the industry is male dominated. She eventually set up a restaurant along with a team comprising of women who had a history of hardships in their lives. An innovative stance to a social problem, her idea was to establish a restaurant with the objective of continuous improvements and sustainable approaches to benefit the society in general with emphasis on women, pushing them to take the risks and do things which others might decline.

CASE DISCUSSION

Meera had substantial knowledge and experience of observing and assisting her father with various aspects of his business. She was driven to follow her idea and help other victimised women in the society. She decided to start her own restaurant named "Women's Avenue." She began her venture with 10 other women. Her restaurant Women's Avenue was finally established in 2012. She approached the government for their schemes and projects to promote women entrepreneurship. She got consistent support from YWSED (Young Women Social Entrepreneurship Development Programme) which is a programme launched in India by The British Council in partnership with Diageo in 2013. This helped her hone her entrepreneurial skills.

The restaurant initially did not get a great response from the market. The customers had framed a perception of the people associated with it as being 'victimised'. Meera sought guidance from local NGOs, who suggested her to create awareness around the purpose of Women's Avenue. Meera realized that a celebrity being associated as the face of her venture would help immensely. Since she wanted someone who would also connect with the ethos of her restaurant, she got in touch with an actress who was known for her charitable work.

Results started to show immediately. The restaurant soon started expanding the cuisine it's offered, and also focused on updating the interiors of the restaurant to create a lively ambience. After achieving success from her idea, Meera eventually opened a series of branches of Women's Avenue across Delhi which focused on only one core concept and vision - To focus on upliftment of the condition of women in the society and promote social entrepreneurs.

Being true to her restaurant's positioning allowed Meera to scale up operations and become profitable quickly. She could call herself a true social entrepreneur.

Challenges Faced by Meera

1. Limited access to funding:

A major problem of a business is to get the funds for growth and expansion. Meera arranged funds for the establishment of her business but the problem of limited funds soon became a hurdle in the way of her idea of expansion of her restaurant.

2. Limited skills with employees:

Meera did not even complete her graduation before she started her own restaurant. She lacked entrepreneurial skills and the other women working with her also lacked professional skills required by them for the smooth working of the restaurant.

3. Patriarchal Society:

Meera's parents and relatives were supportive and encouraged and assisted her in setting up the restaurant; but society at large was not readily accepting of a woman social entrepreneur, especially considering her history.

4. Sustainability:

The restaurant needs to continue to innovate to survive in the long run.

CONCLUSION

Solutions for Other Women Social Entrepreneurs

1. Government organization funding should be easier to access.
2. Venture funds and angel funding should be made available to such ventures.
3. Workshops should be conducted to raise awareness.

About the Authors

DR. SANJEEV BANSAL
DEAN, FACULTY OF MANAGEMENT STUDIES
DIRECTOR AND HEAD OF AMITY BUSINESS SCHOOL
AMITY UNIVERSITY UTTAR PRADESH, INDIA

Dr. Sanjeev Bansal is Dean FMS & Director of Amity Business School, Amity University Uttar Pradesh. In an acclaimed career span of about 27 years in teaching, research and consultancy, he has been invited to be a part of several prestigious academic / professional bodies and in his advisory capacity, has steered them to success.

He is an avid researcher and has more than 125 research papers in prestigious journals to his credit. He has authored thirteen books and has guided several research scholars to produce works of immense educational impact.

Apart from his areas of specialization, he also likes to explore and research the vistas of spirituality, management and quality of work life. During his distinguished career he has had many accomplishments and is hailed as an institution builder, a loved teacher and an ardent researcher.

DR. ANUPAMA RAJESH
ASSOCIATE PROFESSOR AND HEAD – CASE STUDY CENTRE
AMITY BUSINESS SCHOOL
AMITY UNIVERSITY UTTAR PRADESH, INDIA

Dr. Anupama Rajesh is Associate Professor and Head, Case Study Centre at Amity Business School, Amity University, India. Her qualifications include Ph.D. in the area of Technology in Education, M.Phil. (IT), M.Phil. (Mgmt.), M.Ed., M.Sc. (IT), PGDCA, PGDBA. She has also been trained for case study writing at INSEAD Paris. She has a teaching experience of about 20 years including international assignments which include a teaching stint at Singapore and training of Italian and French delegates and students. She has written more than 25 research papers and case studies for prestigious international journals and has six books and several book chapters to her credit. She is reviewer of renowned Sage and Emerald journals. Her research interests are Business Intelligence, Educational Technology, Marketing Analytics etc. while her teaching interests are Business Intelligence, E-Commerce, IT enabled processes and so on.

She is an avid trainer and has trained Union Bank of India, NHPC, ILFS, TATA Motors, Bhutan Power Company employees as well as Commonwealth Games Volunteers and army personnel. She is a Master Trainer from Microsoft, Infosys Partner for Business Intelligence and Academic Partner for SAP ERM Sim.

She has recently won the ADMA Research Award. She has also been awarded "Shiksha Rattan Puruskar" and won several Outstanding Paper Awards at prestigious International forums. She also has a MOOC to her credit.

HAVISH MADHVAPATY
HEAD OF RESEARCH
TRAVERSE STRATEGY CONSULTANTS

Havish Madhvapaty has diverse experience across sales and marketing, academia and market research. He is a Ph.D. scholar researching experiential marketing. His qualifications include Microsoft certified Microsoft Office Specialist (MOS) Master, Google Analytics & Google AdWords Certification, and VSkills Certified Digital Marketing Master. He has also been an MBA Gold Medalist and Scholarship awardee.

Havish presently works as Head of Research with Traverse Strategy Consultants, a research and consulting start-up, where he leads a team of analysts, spearheading all research tasks.

He is also a corporate and academic trainer in quantitative analysis, focusing on Advanced Excel and SPSS.

Havish has over 25 academic publications in national and international journals, and has acted as a reviewer for IGI Global. His research assignments for the corporates has been featured regularly in BW | Businessworld, BW | Applause, IMPACT, Pitch and so on.

ANUPAM SEN
FOUNDER
TRAVERSE STRATEGY CONSULTANTS

As the founder of Traverse Strategy Consultants, Anupam is responsible for running all facets of the business. He has a proven executive management track record and over 14 years of experience driving sales growth in firms. His experience includes working for clients in the Media, Automotive and Healthcare sectors along with pro-bono consulting for NGOs. Anupam in the past has had the opportunity of working with Bharti Airtel, Wipro, and Evalueserve; and was also the founding partner of a technology start-up.

Anupam is frequently invited to speak at forums and seminars at various institutions such as Amity University and has been quoted in print media such as "Pitch – The face of Marketing" magazine. He has also been a part of several jury panels for academia as well as corporate events. He co-authored a research paper titled "Exploring Omnichannel Shopper Behavior and Retailer Mind-Set" in International Journal Of Applied Services Marketing Perspectives.

Anupam also serves on the Board of Directors of Next Traverse Ltd, a Joint Venture enterprise based in Dhaka, Bangladesh.